UNDER THE SHI

of

ALBERT RUSSO

UNDER THE SHIRTTAILS

of

ALBERT RUSSO

an alternative biography

by

Adam Donaldson Powell

l'*A*leph

Adam Donaldson Powell

UNDER THE SHIRTTAILS of ALBERT RUSSO

NB. All reviews, photos and texts from Albert Russo's books
are courtesy of Albert Russo.

Published by l'Aleph—Sweden

www.l-aleph.com

ISBN 978-91-7637-401-6

l'Aleph is a Wisehouse Imprint.

www.l-aleph.com

© Wisehouse 2017—Sweden

www.wisehouse-publishing.com

AUTHOR'S ACKNOWLEDGEMENT

While the idea and initiative for this book was my own, it would not have been possible without the active and enthusiastic participation, consent and materials provided by Albert Russo. Not only has he graciously given me permission to reprint private photos, letters, reviews, as well as portions of his books and information from his websites, but he has also personally contributed to my research by allowing himself to be interviewed (sometimes a bit invasively) for countless hours. He is disciplined, persistent and thorough. As I have written previously: "Creating art and literature requires a creative imagination as well as the ability to get things done in a disciplined manner. Live in the moment, and plan for tomorrow."

I salute Albert Russo's openness and his courage, and I dedicate this book to his life partner (Bernard) and to his children (Tatiana and Alexandre).

Special thanks as well to David Alexander for his prologue.

Adam Donaldson Powell

CONTENTS

PROLOGUE

A MEMOIR TO A MEMOIR

by

David Alexander

I FIRST MET ALBERT IN PARIS AT A COMFORT INN ON THE LEFT BANK. It was on Place Blanche off the Boulevard Clichy, near the Moulin Rouge and the belly-flop bars, in one of which drugs had stopped the heart of the Lizard King and from where strangers had carted then dumped the inconveniently deceased rock singer in his apartment's bathtub. It was my wife who'd introduced us, she who'd become acquainted with Russo by way of his frenetic, and global, literary projects. We'd met him down in the hotel lobby. It was a long time ago, but it was only yesterday.

I can still see the three of us sitting there, in the hotel lobby, me facing the plate glass of the window that fronted Place Blanche, looking out into the darkness of the street beyond this clean, well-lighted place, and Albert sitting in a chair to my left, and my wife Sina to my right.

This was in 1992, and it was pure serendipity that landed us, from the apartment building in Brooklyn where Henry Miller once lived, smack in the middle of the streets that Henry Miller had landed in from Brooklyn, where we, Ambleresque innocents abroad, now marvelled at girls in Irma La Douce poses in many a doorway, and for awhile thought that those quaint-looking stores with old, worn frontages and crudely lettered signs were the way all of Paris showed herself.

My wife had insisted that I meet Russo, who she described as a famous French novelist, which I dismissed at first as the hyperbole she attached to the achievements of all her talented friends. She'd added that he'd been praised by James Baldwin, which was great, but the truth was that by this point I'd gotten tired of these meetings she'd arranged. This was right after the fiasco with her dad's old pal from Ohio, Ernest Tidyman, who'd scripted "The French Connection" and had liked my writing, and who was going to trot me around Hollywood, only to inconveniently suffer a fatal coronary before the fact. So this was pure noblesse oblige on my part; meet the French genius and get it over with, a conviction also owing to the day spent in bed with a strange flu probably caught breathing in germs throughout a transatlantic flight.

We'd brought along a then-novel video camcorder, with which Sina, who was always trailing me as self-appointed camerawoman in those days, began shooting the meeting, and then, without my knowledge, sat the camcorder on a chair with the lens cap askew, and the camera ostensibly turned off, but really on, so that later we could review the entire thing in our room. How sneaky was that? Obviously this was a long time before the word "selfie," with all it implies, was coined; people weren't used to being on camera all the time and to just set up the camcorder and tape for an hour or two would have been considered impolite, or even weird.

And that was that. Russo and ourselves parted ways, night turned to day on the Left Bank, and my wife and myself returned to Henry Miller's apartment in Brooklyn. But that wasn't that, not quite.

An envelope soon arrived in my mailbox. It contained the first of a stack of books, manuscripts, and other publications, that have found a home on one of my library shelves. This was a manuscript for Albert Russo's novel Mixed Blood, which I had promised, with some reluctance, to try to pitch to US publishers. Until that point I hadn't read any of Russo's literary output, yet as I scanned the manuscript, I knew that despite our differences, his dedication to writing was a powerful force that united us. Baldwin's praise, or anybody's else's for that matter, meant little to me. The novel spoke for itself. Russo's work showed me an author who poured out dark secrets and lustrous truths surely dredged from the depths of his being, for in it there was nothing fake or contrived. Mixed Blood had a dreamlike quality about it, not quite Proustian, but of a kindred nature, and it possessed a certain way of walking up the walls of the mind, that I found irresistibly engrossing. It was, to quote Russo's Zapinette, a "masterpizza."

As the years went by, and more of Albert Russo's works were added to my growing library of his books, the author himself took on some of the defining qualities of a character more dreamed than real, even as my own life seemed to grow more to resemble something I had invented in a novel and peopled with characters wholly fictitious. Time would pass without word from Paris … and then there was an email or a phone call, or a new work to be read and commented on.

Then Russo would swim out of view again, but with a strange, imperceivable, yet tangible rhythm, he'd reappear; now with me playing the role of visitor to his hotel in Manhattan, next with a midnight meeting on a railway platform of the Gare de l'Est in Paris, where Russo, bearing two bottles of good wine, hastily arriving at my deliberately sudden invitation, and unaware that my train was the Venice-Simplon Orient-Express, betrayed the irrepressible envy of an inveterate globe-trotter who may have been for once upstaged. More recently, Russo surprised me in turn by relocating lock, stock and laptop, to Tel Aviv in the wake of the Charlie Hebdo massacre after half a lifetime spent as a Paris denizen.

In the following alternative biography, "Under the Shirttails of Albert Russo", he speaks with some reproof of the French in branding him as a rootless person, yet I recall that he wrote, in I-Sraeli Syndrome, concerning "the existential qualm for which my heritage is responsible: Africa, Judaism and Italy. They clash and coexist in cycles, in a fashion so inchoate that I am never quite sure which will take the upper hand."

I for one would counsel Russo to remember Vishnu, who dreamed the universe itself, and to wear his differences as a coat of many colors.

For now, as then, I view Russo as the outsider in virtually every respect, including being an outsider to corporate publishing. I saw this ur-nature as the foundation stone of his life and his work, certainly of his signature work, "Mixed Blood", and again for a recent and very soulful novel, titled "And There Was David-Kanza".

He began life as an outsider; the offspring of refugees to Africa from Nazi and fascist persecution then became an outcast via his self-proclaimed "gaytude." Later in life, as an expatriate in all but having an actual country to be expatriated from, Russo was an outsider even in Paris, his home city of many years, and a literary expatriate in many ways as well. But so, in my own humble way, am I. And I admire Russo for treading the path he's chosen, or in recognizing that it's chosen him.

A few years ago, I drove Russo around Brooklyn by night. Russo understood and could appreciate the desolate beauty in the dense shadows that swarmed beneath the Palookaville Avenue Elevated as I took him on a nocturnal ramble. The desolate spaces broken by the intermittent percussive rumbling of trains rolling across the El's overhead tracks as they pulled in and out of stations, the shuttered frontages of pocket factories and small garages, the purple neon exploding from a midnight taco joint, shouts in Spanish as a brouhaha broke out in a Mexican pool hall, the deepening palpable howling naked loneliness as the El stretched toward Coney Island and rain began to fall and the few stray lights that had been our lodestars faded out entirely in the drizzly blackness. I knew he saw and appreciated these bleak wonderments as much as I.

No surprise here, I think. The external world is often just a mirror. Russo's novels seem more and more to delve into the heart of his own darkness in telling the stories of his life, even if some of them are allegorical, or lightheartedly told, such as those chronicling the saga of that Malapropesque naif with the wisdom of Solomon and the tongue of Voltaire, Russo's irrepressible Zapinette, whose latest appearance in his "Gosh Zapinette", gives us more of the addictive yet acerbic wit of "Zapinette Video", "Zulu Zappy Does the Rainbow Nation", "Zapinette Baguette & Tagliatelle" and others in the series. Yet, serious fiction and biographical memoirs like Russo's poignant biographical memoir "Mamica Mia", have the power to stir the soul, and though there is humor here too, it is often tempered with pensive longing.

As "David-Kanza" tells, as "Mamica Mia" reveals, and as Russo has related to me personally, his family origins were solidly bourgeois. He comes not from artists or artisans, but from hardworking businessmen, even factory hands. I think perhaps that Russo and I could co-manage a repair shop under the Palookaville Avenue El, and learn to like it better than writing. Well, maybe.

About a week after driving Albert around Brooklyn, I walked with Albert around Manhattan. We tripped the light fantastic and generally perambulated through Chelsea and into the Village, then we walked around the Village too. In high school I used to cut class, take the subway train that still runs above the fray of Palookaville Avenue, and get off at West 4th Street and Avenue of the Americas to commence (it seemed then) a sort of Hesse-esque Journey to the East.

There were still head shops around then—the real thing, festooned with flower power Day-Glo paint jobs. I still have a trinket of tarnished silver I bought in one of those long ago. It looked like some stoned version of a G.I. dog tag. Only recently I stumbled onto the fact that it's the symbol found emblazoned on the tomb of Archimedes of Syracuse, the sphere embedded within the cylinder, a symbol of universal perfection. I still wear it sometimes. I've never cleaned it. I prefer the tarnished silver to the new. Perfection does not always seem to shine.

Russo, of course, didn't know any of this as we walked downtown along Fifth Avenue, into a nocturnal street scene full of jeu d'esprit and low-fat mayonnaise, a yup-yup version of City of Night that somehow made me mentally loop the song "Fifth Avenue Heartache" – probably as a form of self-inflicted punishment. The cordoned off streets near Herald Square, void of all but foot traffic and blazingly lit by mobile klieg lights, courtesy of City Hall and the taxpayers who lived on dark streets in the four outer boroughs, seemed then a Mephistophelian backdrop to a lunar circus.

Someday I'll show Russo more of the real City They Named Twice. Someday I'll take Russo walking along Palookaville Avenue Beyond the El, where the dark-skinned men in shalwar kameez, late of Karachi and Islamabad, also mill around beneath the wan light of street lamps with the subway, now submerged below the pavements of Palookaville Avenue, rumbling amidst the earthen bowels of Brooklyn. These are men who reminded Russo of their feral brethren in La Ville-Lumiére, but whom in Brooklyn are just victims like the rest of us, no more, no less. One day I'll show him the Pennycandy Stores of Ferlinghetti (there have always been three of them since as far as I can recall, and they stand there today, just beyond the El where the poet put them, but their owners now speak Hindi and their wives, sometimes also behind the counters, wear the chador).

Russo also knows nothing of that which I can discern. But why should he? I live here, and he does not. Yet he still knows all about it because he understands one fundamental thing above all; the difference between civilization and anarchy, even the difference between samadhi and namparshespa and spiritual death and rebirth, and also symbol and meaning – lo, even the hardest of all to fathom; that between transgression and absolution.

His knowledge of such matters is something like the Dalai Lama's, in fact. Just as I am the Dalai Lama to my hardworking mechanic friends with repair shops on Palookaville Avenue, so Russo is the Dalai Lama to me. He, after all, bears the seven seals and signs of Bodhisattva-hood from birth, while I pal with palookas and skid across the glare ice that lurks beneath the rutted treads of mere existence.

This is what I meant when, some time ago, I coined the phrase "A crystal in a shock wave" that became, with my blessing, the title of his collected works, "Crystals in a Shock Wave".

I confess that I was thinking of myself, not of Russo at the time. Yet I realized that somehow the phrase applied to him as well as to myself, and I used it as follows in my critique of the collection itself: "Like crystals forming in a shock wave, the subjects of [Russo's] stories frequently undergo rapid and complete changes of state, and they are often greatly distorted in the aftermath of the sudden onslaught, or even smashed altogether and broken beyond repair. … In some ways I see Albert Russo as a kind of shaman or holy man. Writing is simultaneously his religion and the cross to which he's nailed. He walks a path through a labyrinth, searching for truth, and he does not fear the distant snorts and echoes of cloven hoofs that may signal the presence of a Minotaur in the maze."

There are levels within levels, stages within stages, truths within truths, dreams within dreams, and lies nestled within the freshly plowed furrows of greater lies waiting to spring into jungles. To my knowledge, the Dalai Lama has never been to Brooklyn. But I have been to Tibet. And I know the Dalai Lama is Albert Russo. What's more, I know I too, am Russo.

PART ONE

ALBERT RUSSO:
FROM THE SOUL OF AFRICA

JAMES BALDWIN: *"Dear Albert Russo: I've read everything you sent me, and I like your work very much indeed. It has a very gentle surface and a savage under-tow—the fiction—and I applaud the wicked portrait of Ionesco. You're a dangerous man. My friend, the Black woman novelist, Toni Morrison, knows what you are talking about."*

These illustrious words by the acclaimed literary giant James Baldwin were written to Albert Russo, in a letter in 1987, just before he died, regarding "Mixed Blood" and other works. The complete letter follows at the end of Part One.

Mr. Russo's novels based on life and events on the continent of Africa are amongst his most celebrated works, and truly represent his first leap into literary excellence. These works include: "La Pointe du Diable", "Mixed Blood" and "The African Quatuor".

"La Pointe du Diable", Russo's anti-apartheid novel which was based on a true story and was subsequently banned in South Africa, was originally published by Pierre Deméyère (Brussels) in 1972, and re-published by Ginkgo (Paris) in 1992 with the title "Le Cap des Illusions".

"Mixed Blood", originally published by Domhan Books (USA), is a novel based upon true facts about an American homosexual who lived with a Congolese 'governess', and who adopted a child of 'mixed blood'. It was later republished as "Adopted by an American Homosexual in the Belgian Congo" by l'Aleph (Sweden) in 2014 (see following paragraph). Prior to the English-language versions, the novel was first published in French as "Sang Mêlé" by Editions du Griot (Paris) in 1990. This popular book was later re-published by France's major book club France Loisirs, and then yet again by Ginkgo Éditeur (Paris).

"The African Quatuor", which includes "Adopted by an American Homosexual in the Belgian Congo" (formerly "Mixed Blood"), "Leodine of the Belgian Congo", "Eur-African Exiles", and "Eclipse over Lake Tanganyika", was published in English by l'Aleph (Sweden)—both as e-books and as separate paperbacks—in 2014. Each of these four novels deals with the three African countries under Belgian rule, and during the post-colonial period: the present DRC (Congo Kinshasa / Zaire), Rwanda and Burundi. "Eur-African Exiles" also deals with Rhodesia / Zimbabwe and South Africa, during and after apartheid. All of these individual novels had been previously published by Domhan Books (USA), and then by Imago Press (USA). The French versions of these novels initially appeared in France as individual books: "Sang Mêlé", "Eclipse sur le Lac Tanganyika", "L'Ancêtre Noire" (later re-published with the title "Léodine L'Africaine"), and "Exils Africains".

Albert Russo is a multilingual author, writing his original works and literary adaptations in English, French and Italian. It should be noted that while he started writing poetry, stories and essays in English (while studying Business Administration at New York University in 1963) in North America, the United Kingdom and other continents, his first published books were in French.

A popular adage in creative writing is: "Write what you know about". Without opening up a hornet's nest regarding this and other so-called "cardinal rules of writing", it is likely most obvious to readers of Albert Russo's novels based in Africa that he knows his subject, does massive research and also possesses tremendous ingenuity in elaborating and embellishing factual incidences into glorious literary expositions—which are both captivating, entertaining and informative. This talent cannot be easily taught in creative writing classes or at universities. It requires an active fantasy as well as the ability to fill in the blanks in stories from the news and personal life history, as well as to create a painterly background with details of the environment, history, politics, flora, fauna, foods, sounds, smells and much more. Albert Russo's novels—especially the ones based on events in Africa—are rich in such descriptive imagery, and they provide every bit of visual and sensorial entertainment as a film or series of photographs.

Albert Russo's first creative expression form was—in fact—photography, and he has taken photographs since he was a young lad. He received his first camera (a Kodak box camera) in 1955, and has published over 55 art photography books with exposés from his travels to exotic places all over the world. Among the awards received for photography books are: Indie Excellence Awards, The Gallery Photografica Award (Silver medal), and the

London Book Festival Awards. In addition, his photos have been exhibited at the Museum of Photography (Lausanne, Switzerland), in the Musée du Louvre, at the Espace Cardin, both in Paris, at Times Square (New York City), whilst his two photography books on Paris and New York have been lauded by Michael Bloomberg (previous Mayor of New York City).

However, the greatest inspiration and tool for Albert Russo's writing was and is his own uncanny ability to constantly co-interact both visually and conceptually with his surroundings, all the while linking fact and fiction inside his mind, and archiving this rich mélange of imagery together with his own experiences of mundane conversations and events suddenly brought to life—until the intensity of it all bubbles and brims over to a literary volcanic eruption which gives birth to both a sense of overall completion as well as inciting in the reader a desire to read, smell, see and hear even more. In short, Albert Russo is a master of story-telling, armed with a poet's tongue and the eyes of a photographer.

But how does Africa fit into his life and literature? Albert Russo's life story is as exciting as his novels. He was born in Kamina, a province of Katanga (Belgian Congo) in 1943, to an Italian Sephardic father (from Rhodes) and a British mother (who had grown up in Rhodesia). He and his family resided in Congo, Ruanda-Urundi and Rhodesia for seventeen years, during which time Albert also traveled often to South Africa. He graduated from high school in Bujumbura, Burundi (Athénée Royal Interracial) on the northeastern shore of Lake Tanganyika. By then he was already multilingual: speaking French, English, Dutch and German (and vernacular Swahili). His many years residing and traveling on the African continent provided Russo with much more than mere local stories to tell. His own family background and social position in a colonialized Africa slowly moving towards independence and coupled with his own thirst and hunger to discover and experience "the soul of Africa" has given way to a plethora of perspectives of historical and literary value, which might otherwise have been lost in the axis of time and change. Albert Russo IS African. Albert Russo IS of 'mixed blood', because blood does not only run in arteries and veins but in the social, cultural and creative DNA as well.

INTERVIEWING ALBERT RUSSO ABOUT
"MIXED BLOOD"

Let us take a closer look at "Mixed Blood" ("Sang Mêlé") and the influences and events in Albert Russo's life which created this fantastic story that has been published and re-published many times by various publishing houses on two continents.

I first read "Mixed Blood" ("Adopted by an American Homosexual in the Belgian Congo") several years ago. Now, upon re-reading the work, I am struck by the notion that the book is actually mostly about identity. The shock of the titled themes "mixed blood" and "adoption by an American homosexual"—no less in the Belgian Congo—in contemporary Western first-world society now seems lessened by social change and human progress. Yes, while we have not come as far as many might wish, we have certainly come quite a way since post-WW2 and the year in which this novel was first published in France (1990). Of course, all literature and art must be seen at least partially in light of the social and political contexts of its era. In that regard, the book was certainly rather shocking. But what about the more universal concepts and ideas that transcend epochs? The book does indeed deliver in a larger time frame as well—through the pervading and underlying universal theme of search for identity in a great sea of currents and elements (natural and not) which lead us, hinder us, and ultimately contribute to our self-definition and the ways in which we shape our lives ... sometimes by way of our choices, and at other times in response to survival (eg. physically, mentally, socially and spiritually). We are all essentially co-creators of our states of mind and being, and always on the lookout for guidance, agreement and support for our ideas and choices. That guidance can come from various sources: religion, laws and regulations imposed by authorities, the media, families, friends and other social groups and institutions ... and authors and artists. The latter can oftentimes see themselves as on the front lines in the war of minds. Sometimes as teachers and propagandists, but more often taking on the burden of encouraging and provoking the public to use their minds in expanded ways, to continue developing, and to become more accepting of one's own need to live and think more creatively, and with fewer restrictions and personal boundaries. This vital and sometimes "dangerous" role as a provocateur requires courage and the willingness to confront one's own perceived limitations. This because in order to inspire introspection in others an author/artist must identify with humanity in ways that are believable and convincing. This is one of Albert Russo's greatest strengths as an author. In all of his books he creates a mysterious mélange of personality confluences and interconnections, stories within stories, voices becoming other voices, and historical references that retain their relevances across decades and centuries.

In "Mixed Blood" there is an abrupt change of "first-person dialoguers", eg. from Léo the son, and then, halfway through the book, to his father as he reads and reacts to a letter from Léo. At first reading, this literary mechanism might seem to be a simplified way of showing generational voices. In fact, I suspect that there was more going on in the mind of Albert Russo when he penned this work. It is, indeed, logical that by using the first-person the author is perhaps freer to become Léopold—more directly and with aplomb—while accessing his own experiences from life. Russo has a child's genius when it comes to being inquisitive and at the same time omniscient, often noticing and dwelling upon small quirks that adults try to ignore but which children (rightly so) find quite significant, eg. the twitching of a person's Adam's apple. By writing as Léo in the first-person (just as he writes as Zapinette in several books in a later series) he is thus free to re-access these memories and fascinations that most of us dismiss and forget as we get older.

Russo's employment of stories within stories (eg. Mama Malkia's folktale, which adds an important psychological layer to an otherwise mundane relationship between herself, Harry and Léo), and his juxtapositions of other less significant stories within the main story, all serve to give the book great depth and a wider net reach in which to capture and maintain readers' interest. At times these well-written sub-plots function as short stories in their own right.

And then there are many underlying sub-themes which are mentioned briefly but in contexts which make them larger than life and utterly spell-binding, such as when a cut diamond is turned slightly to capture life from a different angle. These include, among others, American fascination with a perhaps glorified vision of Africa, Africans' identification and sympathies with American Blacks not feeling free, homosexuality/pederasty, Blacks vs. Arabs, Blacks' sympathy for Jews, African local culture vs. Christian institutions and morality, witch medicine vs. European medicine etc.

I have asked Mr. Russo to write me regarding many of these thoughts and questions, and also to explain the appeal of this book both then, and now. This is his rather candid response:

"I finished writing MIXED BLOOD, my first major African novel, in the Summer of 1986, and sent it immediately to James Baldwin, whom I met soon thereafter, for he had liked it very much. While in Paris we had dinner together and I accompanied him to a private showing of the film 'Lady sings the Blues' (Billie Holiday), of which, he had already penned a scathing review in America. He then kindly invited me to St. Paul de Vence in southern France, but unfortunately he died at the end of 1987, and it was too late. My second stay in the USA after Stonewall (not while I was studying there during Kennedy's presidency) has probably influenced me to tackle the subject of homosexuality, which I had never done before.

"I wrote the novel first in English and had won the Best Fiction Award by Volcano Review in California for the whole first part. Then I showed the English novel to Robert Cornevin, the president of ADELF (association of French-speaking writers) who told me that I absolutely had to translate it into French, so I rewrote and adapted it almost verbatim—you do know that I NEVER translate my books from English into French and vice-versa, I rewrite them, changing all the typical expressions of language A, as well as certain 'images', which I deem untranslatable. Professional translators are not allowed to do what I do. In certain cases, as in 'I-sraeli Syndrome', the English text is much more erotic than the French one, so yes, in some cases, there are additions. I feel freer to express myself in English than in French. 'Ambiance oblige'. When the first French edition came out it was both a critical and a commercial success—all is relative, but that is the book with which my literary career was launched in the French-speaking world.

"The Black-American struggle had a definite impact on my writing. Not only because I have lived in the United States for a total duration of 8 years, two decades apart, but because I was born and grew up in an African colony, where there was racial discrimination. I had read quite a few white and African-American writers, and was well aware of the history of racism in North

America. Yet, if I had to publish the same novel for the 4th or 5th time today, I wouldn't change a word, because I deem that my story is still valid today, maybe not contemporary in Scandinavia or in Holland, but definitely in France—and here, I don't even mention the countries where you get jailed or, worse, decapitated if you are openly homosexual; and even though marriage between partners of the same sex is allowed, there are still millions of people demonstrating every year against that law and against same-sex couples having children. Homophobia hasn't disappeared, and especially not in the French provinces. There are many more gay youths committing suicide than heterosexual teenagers. And something I never heard proffered out loud in the Belgian Congo (yes some of the people were hypocritical all right, but they never dared express those insults publicly) such as 'Sales Pédés' or 'on te fera la peau', which so many young Muslims today shout in the streets when they happen to see two men holding hands. The irony of it all is that in Muslim countries homosexuality seems to be the norm (but you must never mention it). I know, I have been to the Maghreb countries and to Turkey many times. It seems paradoxical, but in my novel, i.e., in the Belgian Congo, gay people were not menaced as they are today. Of course, they were much more discreet too. That may also be the reason.

"I often use the first person vs the third person in my novels in order to better identify with the protagonist and with the other main characters: I am that character, and feel freer to delve into his or her anima.

"Since the very beginning of my 'career' I have liked to include foreign words and expressions. Actually, I'm an African gifted with a number of languages, each being a planet in its own right. Africans have a natural gift for languages. Not only do they speak their own dialect, but they also often speak one of the continent's main languages like Swahili, plus the colonialist's lingua franca: English, French, Spanish, Portuguese … Example: in Burundi, they speak Kirundi, Swahili and French; and those who go to university add English as well into their curriculum. This gift for languages was totally ignored during the colonial period! In France I've often been told that I have no roots. My answer: You are wrong. Compare me to that tropical aquatic plant whose roots develop out of the water (yes, indeed, upside down—ask a botanist and s/he will give you the latin name for this plant / tree). In America that wasn't a problem. Only the French are Cartesian to the point of being intolerant.

"*Please note, dear readers, that from now on I shall use my own neologism 's/he' instead of 'he or she'.*

"*These are the themes that contributed to the success of this book: homosexuality, racial and cultural differences, plus the colonial and post-colonial era. I must insist on this: I went to Senegal (West Africa) about seven years ago and found the very same atmosphere, with the exception that the country was independent, and that they had computers and mobile phones. But in the countryside, I felt exactly the way I felt when I was a teenager in the Belgian Congo and in Rwanda-Urundi. With the major difference that now we were on an equal footing. But all the other problems remained the same.*

"*I'd like to point out the fact that I am not, nor have I ever been a gay militant. I'm just an author like many of my better peers, since I write all kinds of stories, stories which have nothing to do with gay themes. My family read all my novels and they knew very well who I was, including my mother, sisters, children and now grandchildren. They accept me with no questions asked, as well as my partner of 25 years, Bernard, whom they all like very much.*

"*I never liked labels, and that is because of French intolerance: to them I am not an African, since I am not Black. The fact that I write in several languages, disturbs them and they—the big publishers—prefer to ignore me. What is this Albert Russo, they ask, who's lived in Africa, then in America, then in Italy and who speaks French like a Frenchman? He is 'nothing', has no roots. In other words, in their eyes I'm a bastard—in the sense that I am too 'mixed'; they might add, 'too mixed-up'.*

"'*Mixed Blood' has always been very well received in Africa/the Congo, and this hasn't changed. Actually, all my African books are being studied at the University of Lubumbashi (formerly Elisabethville) and probably in the other major Congolese, Rwandan and Burundian universities, both in the History and Literature departments. That makes me very proud. My English versions are also read in Ghana, Nigeria, where Chinua Achebe published some excerpts in his own magazine, and in South Africa, where "Zulu Zapinette" was also published, not long ago.*

"*I have been asked if I intended this story to be a novel. No, I never plan anything. I started writing and this book became a novel.*

"*Robert Cornevin, of whom I spoke earlier, read the original English manuscript and he enthusiastically prompted me to write a French version, which then became a success. Don't ask me how or why it was first published as a book in French. Publishers worldwide—and here I include the 'big' American and British publishers—are irrational, they can even be commercially wrong, but they will never admit it. A bon entendeur salut!*

"I've also been asked how long it took me to write this novel. I'm a slow writer: I need a whole year for a book of 180 to 250 pages.

"When I started writing 'Mixed Blood' there was no Internet. I did a lot of research, the old way. I have read maybe 100+ books on African History, mores, tribal life, oral and written literature, pre-colonial, colonial and post colonial periods. I have read well-written and balanced books, as well as very badly-researched books, especially by Anglo-Saxon so-called 'renowned experts', who are terribly biased, even today, especially where Belgian rule in Africa is concerned. They insist on focus upon the personal and often ruthless rule of Léopold II, who used foreign, British, French and Belgian mercenaries, but also Stanley, the Welsh-American explorer-reporter, who drew the map of what is today the RD Congo, and whom many contemporary Africans are thankful for, in spite of some of his cruel deeds. After the 'international scandal' the British launched, Léopold II cast aside his 'private' property like a hot rod to the Belgian Parliament, which never wanted a colony in the first place. The British, and consequently the Americans, actually put 'a cross on' the most important period, going from 1908 to 1960—that is when that huge territory, the size of Western Europe, 80 times larger than the new 'mother country', became the Belgian Congo, and when the Belgians began to 'repair' some of the worst aspects inherited by a king they never liked, making of it a 'model colony', with all its bad sides: segregation, white superiority complex, and the positive ones: Africans had the best health service of any colony and free primary schooling was compulsory. They also built the best transportation network: more than 6500 kms of railways, 125,000 kms of roads, a small portion of it being asphalted, the best aviation network of the continent, except for South Africa— all but destroyed nowadays.

"Belgium HAD to grant independence to a territory that was not ready for it—blame the major powers of yore: the US, the Soviet Union, China, France, Britain, and what was then called the Third World, including India, Egypt, the 'freed' North African nations, which forced a puzzled Belgium to subject its colony to the greatest bidders. Actually, they helped throw that wonderful giant

and very advanced 'colony' to the dogs, scaring away the Belgian functionaries, until the whole magnificent infrastructure collapsed.

"NOTE: unlike the North Africans who continue to blame France for its colonial past, the Congolese, Rwandans and Burundians are usually on excellent terms with the Belgians. The Congolese still call them their 'uncles'; an endearing word. In Belgium nowadays, the tens of thousands of Black Africans live and work in harmony with the Belgians. My beloved mother had three African nurses, or better said, dames de compagnie, during the seven years of her illness, who became our dearest friends—which is NOT the case with many immigrants of Moroccan origin. Brussels has become the capital of Islamic terrorism of Europe. And yet, Belgium never colonized Morocco; France did. Explain that to me!

"After the success of my African books I was pigeonholed as an African storyteller, especially In France and in Belgium, but not in the English-speaking world. The French publishers of my African novels refused to publish my 'Zapinette series' or my short-stories in French. I had to look for other small and middle-sized publishers for the latter. The owner of Ginkgo, in Paris, for instance, tells me that 'Zapinette' has nothing to do with Albert Russo!!!

"I write my own adaptations in French and English. It is mostly a work of transliteration and of re-writing. I can assure you that it takes as much time as writing my original novel.

"'MIXED BLOOD' was the original title of the novel, but, le marketing oblige, my new publisher suggested that I change the title, and I did, naming it 'ADOPTED BY AN AMERICAN HOMOSEXUAL IN THE BELGIAN CONGO (AAHBC)'; and even though it has a 'tabloid' sounding title, I am quite satisfied with it. I want to reach more readers and this is what is important. Actually, the title 'MIXED BLOOD', which is a good title, is too limited in scope, and furthermore, I have discovered in the meantime that a thriller written much earlier had the same title. 'AAHBC' belongs to me... and to me alone.

"Unlike many American or British authors, I write short novels. I don't like to drag on and on, like my Anglo-Saxon peers do, to the point of discouraging me from reading their 400+ page long novels when I reach page 150. Yet, when I am interested, I can read up to 1000+ page books of history, sociology, psychology, and science (made easy) books. While I am, and will always remain,

an Agnostic, I have about 20 Bibles of all denominations, in 5 languages, as well as archaeological books related to the Bible. To me, the Bible, mainly the Torah, which covers 3/4 of the Christian Bible, is the world's first extraordinary Encyclopaedia, with legends, exciting stories, short and long poems, psalms, half-truths, and proven facts. I read parts of it regularly ... as I read Shakespeare.

"I believe that large conventional Anglo-Saxon publishers think that my novels are too short for saleability. That is why I have small publishers for my works in English: they stress quality over quantity. But here again, Random House et al, could make bestsellers out of each one of my novels that form my AFRICAN QUATUOR. Maybe one day a commercial CEO—aren't they now those who decide which novel will be published or not, instead of the literary editors? —will understand that they have missed out on something, or maybe not. So no, it's not about the economy, 'Stupid', it's all about the lack of perception. To conclude this subject, I am thankful for the Internet, which has lent my books a second and even a third life."

—❧—

NEW LITERARY HEIGHTS:
LÉODINE OF BELGIAN CONGO

In LÉODINE OF BELGIAN CONGO, Albert Russo soars to new literary heights, combining poetic prose with dramatic staging and imaging so descriptive that it transports the reader not only to Central Africa some sixty years ago, but also into individual moments and hours broken down and expanded exponentially so as to command full introspective experience—and which are consequently adopted by the reader as one's own. In addition, Monsieur Russo is also an historian and a teacher—thus supplying the reader with important and sundry information, much of which was never known to most readers (or perhaps forgotten), and which is put into contexts perhaps heretofore unimagined. Another rule of writing (or adage) is to "show, not tell". Well, Albert Russo manages to do both with great proficiency. We both see, hear, smell and learn, by whatever means the author deems necessary and useful—and Russo has a rather large and colorful palette that he works from.

The story itself—yet another powerful study of an individual's search for identity and, again, beautifully expressed through the emphatic voice, questioning mind and open soul of an adolescent—is centered around Léodine, who is the daughter of Flemish Astrid and of the American G.I. Gregory McNeil (whom she had met in France during WWII), but who grows up in the Belgian Congo with her mother, after her father died in a plane crash. Astrid eventually falls in love with one Piet Van den Berg. Léodine one day discovers that her family has a "dark secret"—that her natural father had a black great-grandmother, and that she is of "mixed blood". The story further documents Léodine's return to the Congo as an adult, her dismay in seeing the results of the aftermath of the genocide in Rwanda (1994), and her subsequent adoption of a Mozambican boy whom she named after her first adolescent lover—Mario-Tende.

I see in this wonderful novel seedlings of the persona Zapinette—the protagonist and heroine—in Russo's later "Zapinette series". Chapters five and six of this book are excellent illustrations of Russo approaching the philosophical and ethical larger questions in life through the eyes of an inquiring adolescent, as well as his excellent research and poetic prose. Here is an excerpt from the novel:

Chapter Six

The day of the great departure had arrived. Since I had never taken a plane before, I wriggled with an almost delirious excitement the minute the loud-speaker cracked with the announcement that "the passengers bound for Manono, Albertville, Usumbura, Kindu and Bukavu—which old-timers insisted on calling by its Europeanized name Costermansville, or simply Cost, following the Belgian habit of abbreviating city names (likewise, Elisabethville, Léopoldville or Usumbura, were referred to as Eville, Léo and Usa) – please proceed to gate 2 for immediate boarding."

The sound of all those names which, when we drove to the airport on Sundays, just as visitors, usually either made me feel melancholy or slightly annoyed, according to my mood—I still can't fathom why it triggered such a reaction in me—all of a sudden echoed like a brilliant musical score whose notes pitched into a flamboyant crescendo. I then kept repeating the syllables in my head, so as to immerse myself in them, lest they should be forgotten, for even though I knew that I wouldn't visit any of those places, they'd no longer appear as simple dots on the map.

The sleek white and silver Dakota of Sabena, the national Belgian airline which prided itself on having developed Africa's most extensive domestic network, stood there waiting for us, a mere fifty meters from the terminal. It looked like a beautiful and majestic bird at rest, shining in a lofty posture, with wings spread out and beak pointed towards the sky, a sight of perfect harmony.

What surprised then impressed me as we got into the aircraft, was to feel the gradual stiffening of my calves and the shortening of my breath, as when one begins to climb a hill, since from afar, I had not expected the plane to be so sharply inclined. As a matter of fact I almost lost my balance, so impatient I was to gain the row of seats in the front of the plane, to which the steward was motioning us, while at the same time sporting a broad welcoming smile. In spite of my haste, I noticed how delicate his hands were, and I'd swore they were manicured for I had never seen a man before with nails so neatly cut and so incredibly glossy.

There weren't very many passengers—I thus assumed that the DC3 would unload some of them then pick up others along the route—and we consequently were given permission to choose any seats we liked, ignoring those marked on our boarding tickets.

My mother insisted that we move as far away from the wings as possible, because of the vibrations, which, she informed us, disturbed her a great deal, despite all the Dramamine pills she had swallowed before leaving home.

I was far too excited to waste my time with such preoccupations, and, like a kitten curling up in its new litter, I probed my padded orchestra seat, squirming this way and that before I finally settled—wasn't I going to be lifted into the stratosphere and be regaled with the most unique show of my life, listening to the sweetest music there ever was, the rumblings of our DC3? Then too, I had a window all to myself, since I was separated from Piet and my mother by the cabin's single aisle.

A few minutes later, the steward came towards me and, bending his slim torso, buckled the safety belt around my tummy, too loosely I thought, but surely he was the expert and he knew best. As he did this, a potent whiff of eau de cologne emanated from the upper part of his body and engulfed me. It was at once exquisite and dizzying, so much so that I suddenly had a burning desire to press my lips against his cheek, and the thought made me blush. Then, somewhat miffed, I asked myself, why on earth did people sprinkle perfume on themselves if their neighbors had to keep at a distance. Wasn't that a sort of provocation?

When the steward walked away to attend to the other passengers I became aware of the stronger odor that pervaded the cabin, it evoked the aroma of tobacco leaves laid out to be dried in the sun, mixed with that of warm, opiated leather, almost alive, as if it originated from some game animal that had been just recently killed.

I was floating amid clouds of heady scents, even though we were still aground. But as if reading through my mind, the aircraft suddenly bolted forward and began to hug the tarmac with such fury, under the thrust of its engines, that I felt as though every cell of my body was being shaken and tossed in a zany merry-go-round. It was now pulling me away from earth's gravity with a power that could only be called superhuman. My dreams, at last, were materializing, in a fashion which, if you were not prepared, would have been terrifying. But I was relishing every jolt of our DC3, every squeak of metal, every screech of the tires, and every vibration of the cabin that responded to the captain's orders up in the cockpit, as if he were conniving with God. I was submitting myself to this violence, blindly, wholeheartedly, with an almost frantic sadism, ready even to add my part should it be requested from me.

My mother kept her eyes closed whilst she held Piet's hand firmly, and I could see, the poor thing, how tense she was, gritting her teeth and balling her free fist, with her head tilted back against the cream-colored apron which was tied to the head-rest. I could have bet that she was praying for our plane to carry us safely throughout the trip. What she deemed to be an ordeal, was for me the most exhilarating experience of my life, and the surrounding din which must have sounded to her like hell's pandemonium, splitting her brain, had the opposite effect on me, in that it only bolstered my excitement.

A strange thought then crossed my mind: what if suddenly the Dakota's twin engines both failed at the same time and the aircraft crash-landed in the middle of the jungle? I'd heard someone mention, a few months earlier, at the radio, about an incident involving a DC3 whose two engines had been accidentally turned off, and which in spite of it, managed to glide its last leg without a hitch until it reached the next airstrip.

Playing deity, I imagined that we'd come out miraculously almost unscathed from the fall, whilst the plane would have broken apart, without catching fire. We would then use the cabin, or what would be left of it, as our makeshift abode, until we'd find some generous soul to rescue us. I then pictured those Pygmies of whom Tambwe spoke with a grin of contempt. He would ask me why I was so interested in the lot of such petty, half-sized people, who, according to him, were very primitive, compared to the Bantu race, of which he was a proud member. "As a matter of fact," he would add, "the colonial administration doesn't even take them into account, since they neither live in the cities nor in our native villages. And furthermore, you won't ever see them be conscripted into the Force Publique (the African police), which employs a good number of men from the Lulua and the Bakuba tribes, who have the reputation of being fierce and dependable warriors. And you will certainly never find them working as clerks or even in more menial tasks in government offices." To justify his low esteem of the Pygmies, Tambwe would go on to explain that you couldn't trust them, since they were sly and inveterate liars, but that they were left in peace to roam the jungle, for they could be useful to the Bantu. He admitted that they were good hunters and that they produced excellent wicker baskets which they bartered against metal pots and pans and other civilized utensils.

In the Encyclopedia of Belgian Africa, I'd read that more than two thousand years before Christ, Pharaoh Pepi II had dispatched an exploratory escort to Central Africa, as far as the Ituri region, in northern Congo, with the purpose of finding the Nile's source, and that, after that first military expedition, one of his generals had come back to Egypt, accompanied by a small group of Pygmies. Pharaoh stood in ecstasy before those "midgets hailing from the tree country", and he ordered his guards to take special care of these very strange and very unique guests, requesting that they be given all the food they wanted and that they never be disturbed in their sleep, for fear that the evil spirits would cut down even further their already diminutive size, on top of which, he was convinced that they were the 'dancers of Ra', the Sun God. The Egyptian priests even claimed that only the crowned cranes would dare confront the 'fairy people', since those aristocratic birds were regarded as deities.

When visiting Luxor, you may find Pygmies silhouetted on temple reliefs or pictured in some of the tomb frescoes, under the name of 'Akka'. More amazing still is the fact that, after thousands of years, the Akka continue to live in the

Congo's Ituri region, albeit in very small numbers. Nowadays, the Bantu refer to them humorously as the Tiki-Tiki tribe. But unlike the latter or the peoples of Sudanese descent, they have maintained their ancestral way of life that goes back even prior to the invention of the wheel, agriculture and farming. They still wear, as their only garment, the 'tapa', a narrow swath of ficus bark, which they decorate, using charcoal, around their waist. And whereas most Africans and Whites consider the jungle to be a dreadful place fraught with all sorts of dangers and mysteries, they deem it as their foster-mother, inasmuch as they don't believe in spirits, good or evil.

The male Pygmies spend most of their time hunting with bows and arrows, their traditional weapons. They also catch animals in traps, or using nets, copying thus the Bantu. They generally hunt small game or fowl from a hide, but they also go, rarely, it must be stressed, after formidable preys, many times their size, such as buffaloes, or even leopards and elephants. Only the more agile and dexterous venture here, lest they be torn apart or crushed to death.

The women tend to the family hut and the cooking, over firewood; at other times, they search for fruit, edible roots and mushrooms, as well as insects and frogs. To vary their diet, they also go net fishing along a spring or a river in the vicinity of their hamlet, all the while they keep chewing 'dawa' (hallucinogenic herbs) to give them courage. Yet no season is more auspicious than that during which they collect honey.

At sundown, the men start singing in praise of God, showing thus their gratitude to 'Mungu' for His goodness and for His bounty. This daily ritual is usually followed by dancing, they hop in circles or march in Indian file. They do it with such joy and such fervor that their Bantu customers sometimes invite them to perform in front of them and celebrate the closing of a deal.

Pygmies are by nature nomads and they set up camp wherever there is game to be hunted, though they never cross the boundaries of the chiefdoms belonging to their Bantu customers, mainly for two reasons, the first one being obviously economic and the second one to gain the latter's protection. The little men barter game meat, which they customarily bring smoke-dried—thus prepared, the meat doesn't rot so quickly in the sweltering heat -, as well as the produce of their recent crops, and artefacts such as wicker baskets, against manufactured objects only the Bantu can offer them. And to exceptionally good customers, they yield their ivory, as a proof of allegiance.

The Bantu consider them to be their private property, or even their slaves, even though the little men secretly think otherwise, for they feel so free that, without warning their customers, they can leave overnight as their interest and their fancy guides them, and head for another region, next to a new village.

In the Pygmy society, everyone, adult and child, contributes to the life of the group, performing tasks that don't follow any strict rules, so as not to disrupt the collective harmony, reigning in their midst. Such an egalitarian utopia, which goes back to prehistoric times, may appear idyllic, yet it is their only alternative for survival. Unlike the animistic Bantu, the Pygmies believe in a single God, who is at once their benefactor and the protector of their children. When one of them is wounded or dies, they celebrate Him with offerings, in order to appease His wrath and regain His benevolence.

Along the centuries, many of them have mixed with the Bantu and the Sudanese and they have consequently become like them, sedentary, tilling the land and acquiring new skills. They, of course, are somewhat taller than their brethren, who kept away from the process of miscegenation.

Tambwe, one day, came and told me a funny story regarding "one of those foxy and scheming midgets". A village chief, presumably a distant relative of his, once mocked a little man who had proudly presented him with a large wicker basket and a dozen arrow points which he had made himself, in exchange for some salt and used metal bowls.

"Tsst, tsst," sniggered the chief, "you pretend to be a man because you can weave a few rotten strings and catch some miserable forest bugs! What a joke! A real man is one who pays taxes, my boy. And I've never heard that either your wife or your parents have paid any taxes lately. Why do you think the colonial administration doesn't even bother to collect them from you people? For the simple reason that they consider you like children. That's why."

The poor Pygmy remained aghast for a while, then, still keeping mum, he vanished into the brush. He came back a few days later, accompanied this time by three of his buddies. They were all carrying some game meat: an antelope, a warthog and half a dozen partridges, freshly slaughtered. They headed directly towards the only store of the village and haggled with the owner, convincing him to pay them in money. Once the deal had been settled they walked to the chief's hut and said to the startled patriarch: "Here are your taxes, Sir! Are we now not worthy to be called real men?"

33

We had left Kindu, which lies on the banks of the Lualaba river, a mere half an hour when we entered a zone of turbulence, so sudden and so violent it was—the aircraft jolted like a wisp of straw in a whirlwind—that I felt as if I was going to be dismembered by some invisible hand which had introduced itself inside my body, without any warning, unobtrusively, but not before twisting each one of my limbs and squashing them into a bloody pulp.

This time, I didn't appreciate the plane's antics one bit, and even less its stupid rattle or its long-drawn wails that reminded me of a stalking old beast in its final stage, being tracked down by a big game hunter. I felt so sick I almost wished it would crash and end the racket. But, unable to avoid the atmosphere's murderous air pockets, the DC3 continued to swing wildly and haphazardly. I could never have imagined that a maiden flight over the equator could be such an ordeal. All kinds of objects were knocking against each other in the baggage compartment or flying around the cabin like unguided missiles, some of them falling right on top of the passengers' heads. It was such an ineffable mess: here a plaid landed on the shoulder of a lady, there it was a heavy leather valise, falling over the bare legs of a child, who began to scream, still farther away, a toilet bag scattered its contents all over the aisle. I even saw a fishing rod hit a couple across the face with such a vengeance, that they remained dazzled for a minute before they reacted.

I then cast a furtive glance in the direction of my mother, almost cautiously, as if this new effort might cost me a dislocation of the neck. Her face had turned ashen and, holding a comfort bag to her mouth, she tried in vain to throw up. Piet soon extracted a small flask from the inside pocket of his jacket and rubbed some eau de cologne over her forehead and her cheeks. Not to become sick myself, I looked away and caught sight of the steward who was busy serving a snack to a couple, sitting three rows in front of me. The man was trying to take a sip from the cup of coffee he'd just been offered but another jolt of the plane made him spill the steaming liquid over his knees whilst his wife heaved a sigh of despair and bent her torso against the back of the seat opposite her. As for the steward, his complexion veered from white to yellowish, so much so that I thought he might roll his eyes up and faint any minute.

He was gesturing like an acrobat, trying to maintain his balance. He nevertheless managed to hand a comfort bag to the lady, who immediately vomited all the food she had ingested during the previous hours. As she emptied herself, she accidentally pushed away the sandwich with the still *untouched glass of orange juice that stood on her tray, it came down, trickling along her stockinged leg.*

I was stunned when, the aircraft having resumed its smooth journey, Piet informed me that we had dropped fifteen to forty meters in those ghastly airpockets. Could that be at all possible, without the plane breaking in two? I had a hard time believing it, inasmuch as Piet had added that this kind of incident happened quite frequently over the equator, due to the colliding influx of warm and cool air, whereas the ground humidity oscillated between 65% and 90%. Then only did it dawn on me how lucky we were to live on the high plateaux of Katanga, whose climate was so much healthier.

I was even more convinced of our fortune after we had spent three quarters of an hour in the barracks of what stood as Kindu's terminal and I suddenly longed for the light evening breezes of Elisabethville, for here, the air was so sticky and muggy that I had the impression of being immersed in a huge tank of honey; you'd be short of suffocating as if your nostrils had been instantly glued from the outside.

Thank goodness the stopover in Usumbura was much more bearable, the heat being drier and the atmosphere as translucent as pure crystal. Before landing, the pilot had allowed us a breathtaking view of Ruanda-Urundi's capital, encased between a majestic row of bluish mountains and Lake Tanganyika, which looked more like a sea really, so large was the bay. The handsomely drawn city was lined with wide avenues whose jacaranda and flamboyant trees gave off the sight of a pleasant if dormant location. Never before had I seen a landscape so grand and so magnificent, and for I know not what reason, it made me think of a Pacific island, pictures of which I could recall from several recent issues of the National Geographic, to which Piet had subscribed earlier in the year. An odd thought crossed my mind that we no longer were in Africa and that the cartographers had made a gross mistake, like when, in the Middle Ages, the scientists insisted that the earth was flat. It is so human to believe that elsewhere is always a better place. Here, Europeans were forever dreaming of Paris or of America and, much later on, when I was residing in Europe, I would smile each time people mentioned the Black Continent with almost mawkish lyricism, praising its primitive lifestyle and its laid back mentality. I always wondered why the white folk in Africa considered themselves as second class citizens compared to their peers in Europe, no matter what profession and social rank they belonged to, and this in spite of the fact that they had better

*salaries or earned more money, some having made a fortune in the colonies—
yet unlike the ongoing myth, the latter were far and between. As for the
indigenous people, in what subcategory had they been cast, they for whom
Bulaya (Belgium) conjured up images of the Land of milk and honey, blessed by
perennial rain or snow, during the cold season? Tambwe, for one, had plastered
on the walls of his hut washed out Sabena airline posters of Brussels' famous
Grand-Place, glittering at night with its gold-plated spires and façades, the city's
landmark statue of Manneken Pis, and a snow-covered forest in the southern
region of Ardenne. He would look at them every morning when he got up, as
one looks at a relic, convinced they were different facets of Paradise, and
thinking how the Europeans must feel happy sharing in its bounty.*

BLOOD RUNS DEEPER THAN SKIN COLOR—
ANOTHER INTERVIEW WITH ALBERT RUSSO

And I wonder, what is the root and cause of Albert Russo's fascination with
"mixed blood"? The other questions regarding personal and group identity,
politics, and cultural differences are—in most cases—perhaps rather
comprehensible. Albert Russo is not, himself, of mixed blood—or is he? Is
"mixed blood" perhaps an expression of his own mixed cultural heritage—
or does the author have more to reveal to inquisitive readers who finally
want to know his answer to this question?

I felt compelled to ask Monsieur Russo what is the source and raison
d'être of his previous fascination with "mixed blood", and how this
particular topic was received by readers, the media and publishers at the
time. This is what he has responded:

*"I became convinced that I was of mixed blood during the years of my
secondary schooling in Usumbura / Bujumbura, once I started attending the
Athénée Royal Interracial—where I had white, black and Asian classmates (a
rarity in the colonies, in fact it was exceptional; and now I deem it a privilege
Whites in the other colonies did not have, at least not while I was still a child).
My childhood left me with very bad memories, because of the nastiness and the*

jealousy of my father's Italian-Sephardic family towards my beloved mother—
'the stranger, the foreigner'—who was much better educated than them, who
spoke English—they called her 'la Inglesa'! in a derogatory tone, for it was a
language they couldn't understand, and she who, furthermore, played the piano
beautifully—'who does she think she is, pummeling the piano notes like that,
and giving us headaches with her Chopin, Beethoven and Black American
music?'

"In my own family, I already felt estranged: different languages, different
backgrounds, conflicting cultures. Later on I learned that not only my families
were of different religions—Jewish, Christian, and Animist—but also of
different races, since I also have cousins of mixed-blood (white / black) in the
Congo and in Zimbabwe.

"Going back to my novel MB, later known as AAHBC, my peers, as well as
new students and new professors of Literature who may one day read that novel
or the complete 'AFRICAN QUATUOR', might ask themselves, whether the
protagonist and the other main characters who appear in AAHBC are real, or
come from my imagination. They existed all right. Harry Wilson (not his real
name) was an acquaintance of my parents, but it is only as a young adult that I
understood who he really was: a homosexual. And yes, he did adopt a mulatto
boy (again, Léopold was not his real name). As for Mama Malkia (again, not
her real name), she was one of our cook's two wives, the older one. Bigamy was
not permitted in the Belgian Congo, but my father convinced the colonial
administrator to close an eye, which he did. This is also an example of the
flexibility of the Belgians in the Congo. Whereas mixed marriages were looked
down upon, they existed, and at primary school I remember having had several
mulatto classmates. The latter studied and played with us quasi-normally. Our
teachers condemned any blatant discrimination and punished the pupils who
were caught insulting them. Mixed classes started existing in the mid-nineteen-
fifties, at secondary school and in the brand new and beautiful universities, like
Lovanium in Léopoldville and the University of Elisabethville. This is to show
and to prove the benevolence of the Belgians, compared to all the other
colonialists, whether British, French, Portuguese or Spanish. Which again, does
not mean that the Africans were on an equal footing. Until the mid-fifties, they
were considered 'eternal children'. I should also stress the fact that during the
seventeen years I spent in Belgian-ruled Africa, I have never seen a black man
being hit or thrashed. Those who committed petty crimes were sent to prison for

a few weeks. And yes, they were scared of the 'kaboke' (police), who could also be an African. Here, it is also true that some white people took advantage of that fear and threatened them with calling a kaboke. But never, ever was there anything similar to the KKK in America, lynchings or killings. There had been, before my birth, a few uprisings in smaller towns, and there, the Force Publique did kill dozens of Africans to quash the so-called rebellions. I personally never witnessed such events. I repeat, it is true that the big Belgian and foreign companies earned millions of dollars doing business in the Congo, but it is also true that the majority of white functionaries were not rich people and that the Africans largely benefitted from a health service, second to none (much better than even in rich South Africa, for instance) and free primary schooling for Africans, both in their native tongue and in French. Actually these Africans, under the Belgians, were the best educated of all colonies. The big mistake of the Belgian colonial administration, which unlike the others had no colonial experience and proved to be quite naive, was that it started educating an African elite much later than, let's say the British or the French. This being said, the elites were a tiny minority in the British and French colonies, while the masses of Africans were very neglected, compared to what happened in the Congo and in Ruanda-Urundi. With all theses explanations, I still am a fervent anti-colonialist, but I cannot let people write untruths. The rest of the world, led by the Anglo-Saxons, prefer, even today, to erase the history of the Belgian Congo, and still only refer to Léopold II and to Conrad's masterpiece 'The heart of darkness', which has nothing to do with the Belgian Congo, since it was written during Léopold II's era. I despise liars and so-called 'historians' who claim to be experts on colonialism; many of them are ideologues who distort historical facts. Nothing is ever black and white —isn't that ironically appropriate here?

"The other big irony is that in 1958—only two years before Congo-Léopoldville's Independence, an International Commission came to the Congo and lauded the Belgians for their 'magnificent' work vis-à-vis the African population. Then, when the whole infrastructure collapsed, weeks after the Congo's Independence in 1960, and tribal wars erupted such as I had never before witnessed, the Belgians began to be called the cruelest colonialists that ever existed!!!

"Last, but not least, I wish to conclude on a very personal note. My own father, during his 35-odd years of living in the Congo and Ruanda-Urundi used to spend half of every week in the bush, visiting Africans and Belgians in villages. Often his car broke down and often he was the guest of African chiefs, sleeping in huts and sharing their meals. He could have been killed and no one would have found out how or where. This is to tell you how safe the Congo was, not because of fear, but because they felt protected. I left Africa at the age of seventeen, and I can only remember smiles and good humor. Yes, I can say it: the great majority of Africans were happy with the Belgians, who had eradicated many of the deadly diseases, which have now returned. And yes, today's Congolese live in poverty and sickness such as I had never before seen. In the last ten years, six million+ Congolese have died, either because of tribal feuds, conflicts between rebels and the government forces, or because of illness. The Congo today is also known for having the highest percentage of rapes in the world and the UN—that useless 'grand machin', as Charles De Gaulle justly called it—has sent the largest contingent of any country, spending billions of dollars… and letting people be killed, often taking advantage themselves of the soil's bounty, and raping women. You will never hear or read such facts, because speaking of them is very politically incorrect. Damn political correctness, a terrible and often noxious idea which America spread around the world. Actually, I believe the USA, which has saved Europe and Asia from the Nazis and the Japanese fascists, has committed crimes much bigger than what they say about the Belgians. One crime doesn't excuse another crime.

"I know that what I just wrote will astound and even infuriate university professors around the world, yes even in Africa. I say 'be damned' to whomever treats me as a racist or a colonialist. My Congolese, Rwandan and Burundian brethren are there to defend me, from Lubumbashi to Likasi and Kinshasa— and by the way, they created a Wikipedia page about me in Lingala, one of the five major African languages of that huge country, the lingua franca being French, from Bujumbura to Muramvya (both in Burundi) and Kigali, the capital of Rwanda. Some Hutu and Tutsi still blame the former Belgian administration for their 'divide and rule' policy—the Hutu in Rwanda and the Tutsi in Burundi. This is probably true, but it never was the Belgians who incited the Hutu to kill almost a million Tutsi and moderate Hutu in 1994! Actually, during their administration they never allowed the Hutu and the Tutsi to murder each other.

"Recently I was approached by the BBC for an interview about the Belgian Congo, but they didn't like what they heard since they retained their clichés and untruths, and I thus told them to go to hell. Here we are talking of the so-called prestigious and world respected BBC, which—by the way —did air one of my African stories a few years ago.

"Speaking of clichés, a few years ago, in Oslo, I met a nice Asian reviewer, we sympathized and she gladly accepted to write about LBC. Her comments were very positive, except when she concluded the review with saying that, being a white person, I could never put myself in the shoes of Africans. How wrong she was—with her cliché—of course she didn't know anything about my real background. So I can excuse her.

"A last anecdote—the anti-cliché: At the beginning of the new millennium, a friend of mine living in London, offered MB / AAHBC to the Nigerian Ambassador in Great Britain, who commented: 'Funny that I have never heard about that Congolese writer, Albert Russo—he is probably himself of mixed blood, he knows his subject almost like a historian. Thank you so much.' My friend answered with a smile: 'Yes, he is Congolese, but rather of the pale type.' 'An albino?' 'No … white, with blue eyes.'"

ALBERT RUSSO'S VIEWS ON THE MECHANICS OF HIS WRITING AND ON PUBLISHING

Albert Russo is indeed a very prolific writer. I have asked him to respond to several questions regarding his work routines, publishing experiences with self-publishing and small independent publishers, self-marketing, and his approach(es) to novel-writing. Both wanna-be writers and published authors are often interested in knowing various "tricks-of-the-trade" that established authors employ, as well as the problems they face. Here are some of the questions I have posed, and Russo's responses to them:

- How many hours do you work each writing day? Do you make work routines? Do you ever get up in the middle of the night to write when ideas occur to you? Do you note ideas in a notebook to use later on, that you carry around or have in your home?

Albert Russo's responses:

"As I said before, I'm a slow writer, but I maintain strict discipline and I usually write five days a week, five to seven hours a day, whether I pen one page or more. Right now, having moved to a new country, I can only write a page or two every ten days, which is terribly frustrating, since writing is also a great therapy. I have a file at home with notes and ideas, but I never jot down anything when I am outside of my apartment. What I sometimes do, when I have to wait for a doctor, is write a short poem in longhand, but that's all. Unlike some other writers, I can't create in cafés, libraries or other public places, because people distract me."

- Is much of your descriptive writing (e.g. details about landscape, flora, fauna, foods, smells, politics etc.) from memory, or from extensive research?

"Having grown up in Africa, I have always been moved by the beauty of nature: landscapes, sunsets, fauna and flowers. I remember all these, the instant I think of Africa: the smells, the colors of the trees, the flamboyants, the jacarandas in full bloom. When I tackle politics, I do some research, to be sure I am not writing falsehoods, even if I have a good memory of what happened in Africa."

- Do you work on several writing assignments/projects at the same time (eg. other short stories, poetry, essays), and if so, does your novel-writing inspire these other works?

"I can only concentrate on a single project at a time, whether it is a novel or a short story, or even an essay. The only exception is poetry: I take a break and have to write a few verses; it is sort of an existential need. When I spend too long a time away from poetry, I start feeling uneasy."

- Was it in your original plan to publish the four novels as the "African Quatuor", or was your decision to group them together one that came after all four had been written?

"In reference to my AFRICAN QUATUOR, the decision to reunite my four novels on Africa was a joint decision of my publisher l'Aleph and I."

- Have any of the characters or events in your novels been recognized by the real-life persons they are based upon? If so, what have been their responses?

"My beloved mother, and especially my sisters, recognized everyone in my books, even though I had changed the names. The extended members of my family, i.e. aunts, uncles, cousins, etc. never commented on my writing. It is well known that very close people are sometimes afraid of being depicted in a book. Only one uncle and one cousin, who still live in southern Africa, have read and liked my novels. The rest—about 20 people—have kept mum."

- Do you have editors who assist you with proofreading in English and French? Are those persons employees of your publishing companies? Does bi-lingual writing entail much personal responsibility for editing and proofreading in other languages?

"When I write in French, editors always proofread my manuscripts and they submit their comments to me for approval. In English it was the same with my small and very literary publisher, Imago Press. Otherwise, I am in charge, which is quite a responsibility and a burden. But I prefer it that way, since no one can touch or change what I have written, except for a few lines which a publisher asks me to take out, because I am getting too 'politically incorrect'. Like those 'big' American publishers who demand that you rewrite a book or delete whole paragraphs, or worse chapters, and all of this without any guarantee that, after your excruciating efforts, they will actually accept your manuscript. I deem those editors to be unethical and their decision-makers to be crooks. I have had a horrible experience like that with Flammarion, a major French House. I wrote an essay about that experience in English, and won an award for best journalism in California."

- What are your thoughts and experiences about the possible differences between writing literature to be published on the internet vs. in books? Do your styles differ when publishing for persons who read on-the-run or online in opposition to reading a novel that was originally written in a paper format?

"I don't like to write for the Internet, except when I submit poetry and short stories for contests. When a publisher wishes to publish a whole novel of mine online, I accept it, provided that I get a proper contract. I don't change a word, since I always hope that the ebook will come out in print in the near future."

- You have both self-published and used many small independent presses for publication. Tell the readers a bit about your experiences with both— how much work do you put into editing your own books, and self-marketing? How do you market your books today (book fairs, tv, radio, internet, Facebook, websites etc.)?

"I have had small, average-sized and big publishers, mainly in France. I leave the marketing to the latter two, who, by the way, regularly organize book fairs in Paris, in the provinces and in Belgium, in which I take part. In English I try to help my small publishers, by suggesting ideas. I personally am not good at marketing my own books, even when I self-publish. For this reason, I sometimes buy marketing services, provided they are within my means. I don't know how to use social networks, in spite of the fact that I have Facebook, LinkedIn and Twitter. And I don't like to spend too much time on them, inasmuch as I write in two languages and I correct all my Italian books myself, including after the publisher has edited them. As I said before, at this moment I don't even have the time to write regularly for myself."

- Many of your novels could easily be made into theater plays or films. Do you consciously approach writing novels in a cinematic fashion? Have any of your novels been made into plays or films? Which novels would you like to see onstage or at a cinema? And why these particular ones?

"Quite a few reviewers wrote that some of my novels were good material for the movie industry. My main French publisher has tried to get MB / AAHBC on screen for years, but nothing has resulted from his efforts in that direction. I know that a few novels of mine would make interesting films: actually my whole AFRICAN QUATUOR, LE CAP DES ILLUSIONS, as well as THE GOSH ZAPINETTE! series; the latter one, more for television than for the big screen. But, with the years, I have realized that it is but a dream—unless you have written a bestseller, and even then, there is no connection whatsoever between the Book industry and Cinema. So I have stopped bothering with the idea.

"I do have two of my African novels 'filmed' like documentaries, AAHBC and EAE, respectively 90 and over 100 minutes. But those film adaptations do not interest Hollywood."

PEEKING UNDERNEATH
THE SHIRTTAILS OF ALBERT RUSSO

One of many examples of Russo's "cinematic writing style" describes a pedophilic experience—as if it were a dream. To describe such an experience in this way is not unnatural, as it is quite human to attempt to disregard the horrible validity of such a personal transgression and intrusion through denial that it really happened. Here Albert Russo's protagonist (Léodine) shows incredible strength in analyzing the events, ultimately accepting that they—in fact—did occur, and for a time dismissing it, seemingly without much further ado. But I can only wonder if Léodine became a "feminist" after that experience—perhaps much as her alter-ego "Zapinette". Is it possible that Zapinette is a literary split personality? The "dark secret" that Léodine carries as a burden—that of being of "mixed blood"—in my opinion pales against the burden of this particular secret.

Of course, I have many questions for the author. Not only regarding the source of this writing in his own life (or in that of another person that he has known), but also concerning why and how Léodine was able to survive this traumatic experience. Did her own mother's sexual "looseness"—often accompanied by her abuse of alcohol—enable Leódine to identify with and process this intrusion as "natural" for her—a young woman who is already branded as an undesirable person because she is of "mixed blood"? And even more intimately, knowing that Albert Russo has previously been married and has two grown children whom he loves, how has his "feminism" been affected by and affected his own subsequent homosexual life? These are questions that are perhaps "politically incorrect" and/or "personally improper" to ask of anyone—let alone an author of fiction. But I am going to ask the questions. Here is the excerpt to which I am referring:

Arnaud poured the last drops of the rosé wine into my glass and exclaimed: "Down it in one gulp! This will be the year!"

I don't know why but his gesture gave me a fit of the giggles, and soon the two men joined me in a guffaw. I couldn't put one word after the other, so shaken I was, the situation getting even more difficult when I began to hiccup: "... what are you ... talking about ... I'm ... I'm much too ... young .... to get mmm ... to get married." I couldn't even recognize the sound of my own voice, for it reverberated like that of a ventriloquist's puppet, breaking in the middle of a sentence as if when a soprano, well into her aria, gets interrupted by a sudden attack of asthma, her vocal cords then rasping horrifically.

I conjured up the ridiculous character created by Hergé, the famous Belgian author of Tintin's adventures, Bianca Castafiore, the stout and rambunctious opera singer who was always prone to attract thieves because of her jewels. This last image made me hysterical. From that moment on, events began to jostle in my head and I can only surmise what followed. I can still see these pictures torn to bits like confetti whirling before my eyes. And in the midst of it all, Rupert carries me to my room, helping me undress, so that I can get into my nightie. Then everything gets blurred. I must have been sound asleep when—was it past midnight, or in the wee hours of the morning? -, a manly face, clean shaven and smelling of menthol approaches me. I open my eyes, at least I think I did, and feel his sweet-scented breath on my cheek. The man's features strangely resemble those of Rupert's friend, and he is alone with me in my room. He whispers things that seem to have slipped out of a poetry book, they are so smooth and gentle: "I love your velvety skin .... your hair is pure silk ... I can but kneel at your feet as I kneel before the Virgin Mary ... you're so pure ... my rosebud .... my ..." These words have the lightness and the quality of Brussels lace.

They envelop me like a light breeze and I welcome it wholeheartedly.

Did I actually feel his finger glide over my breasts, then slip downward, further down, drawing circles around my navel? It followed its course, further down still, oh my God! Then, not one but several fingers clasped the upper band of my pantie, and I began to remonstrate. What he was doing to me wasn't right. But his murmurs resumed and this time had the levity of rose petals—it felt as if they whirled above me before they gently landed over my eyelids, like a caress which I could not decently repel. I believe his lips brushed mine, the same way a bee gathers pollen from a hibiscus flower. These same lips then pressed themselves tightly between my thighs, and there I felt a warm and pleasant moistness. Did I wet my nightie? I suddenly gasped, flushing with shame. I dared not open my eyes, lest I shock—the stranger as well as myself. I began to whimper and turned my head from left to right, then from right to left, repeating this gesture obsessively, like an automaton, whose batteries are at the end of their tether, aware that its movements would slow down and gradually cease. And the moment froze. "You mustn't, you mustn't," I kept repeating

45

feebly. "You're ..." I then felt as if someone zipped my lips shut. I was now praying for the man to stop what he was doing, in spite of his being so gentle and so solicitous, but my plea remained unheeded, and worse, or should I say heck, my thoughts began to fly away, far away from the scene, as if what was happening to my body no longer concerned me, or that I had just become a simple spectator. It must have resembled one of those out-of-the body experiences where your mind appears totally split from your flesh. And indeed, I was witnessing the battle my instincts were waging against that foreign element, the adult male, then how they slowly, gradually yielded to the man's fondling, and how the sin of the flesh, so much decried by the nuns at catechism, was taking place under my gaze. Until now it had been so abstract, so often repeated, that it had almost meshed in my mind with the much more trivial and forgettable anecdotes of life. But suddenly, I sat petrified, for without warning, something began to rub against me, at first soft then becoming very hard and taking on a monstrous consistence. It went on rubbing against my thigh, savagely, probing dangerously upwards, seeking an opening, but my body resisted, fighting as if for dear life. I then heard my nightly visitor huff, calmly at first, then with an increasing agitation that bordered on rage. I felt his hot breath on my skin, it was burning. At last he lashed out, holding on to me with a furious energy, and he let out a long-drawn moan, as if someone had just dealt him a terrible blow. And all of a sudden he went slack. God, what was wrong with him? Was he ... dead? Then, to my horror, I became aware of a warm and sticky liquid spreading between my thighs.

The next day, when Rupert knocked at my door – it was past seven and a half – I was still asleep, or rather slumbering, for I didn't want to get up, as if I needed that space of time to dilute into the marshes of my mind those, what were they, memories, rantings, which had given me such a shock? Then, mechanically, my hand went to rest over my loins and I felt so relieved to find that it wasn't smeared. That was enough to discard any residual doubt about what really happened, and I refused to even embrace the thought that I might have gone to the bathroom in the middle of the night in order to wash myself, using a glove. After I brushed my teeth—it took me about ten minutes before I could resume my senses—an incredible brightness filled my head. It was almost like a flood of light invading it, so dense and so powerful, that all the shadows and the particles still clinging to its corners got wiped out, leaving a huge and blinding void in its stead. What was happening to me that my senses were suddenly so exacerbated, so alive? I was seeing everything through a prism of such burning intensity that I asked myself if I hadn't suddenly been bewitched, for every object that surrounded me became highlighted with extraordinary acuteness: my toothpaste flashed with the fluorescence of an advertising neon, my hair seemed to be spangled with a myriad fireflies, I was hearing myself swallowing in stereophonic sound, I could even 'see' and 'hear' my skin breathe as if each pore were a miniaturized loudspeaker, and yet in spite or because of this state, I felt paradoxically numbed, cut from reality. It wasn't out of a sense of fear, or of joy, or even of resentment, no, it was more as if a stranger had slipped into my body, surreptitiously, during the chaotic minutes that preceded my awakening, for I had the impression that my personality had been split, the second me watching over my habitual self with a mixture of indifference and irony. And every so often the intruder would cast me a disdainful and condescending glance, like those self-righteous bourgeois who give you the once-over at a cocktail party, as if to say: "you don't belong here!"

From this point on, the events unfolded at a surprising speed, like a film reel that the cameraman accelerates, botching down some of the things I had lived, as if my mind had wished to erase them.

And here is Russo's response:

"Indeed I am a staunch feminist, and I have always liked the company of women. I despise the gay people who speak of them with disrespect or, worse, with vulgarity, proffering sexual insults in order to demean them. After all, where would they be if there weren't women? It is they who are the sluts!

"I am atypical in too many ways for my own good. I was asexual until the age of 20, yes 20! I didn't even know there was a difference between heterosexuals and homosexuals, let alone transvestites and transgenders. I was so damn naive, whereas my teenaged classmates in Africa were already having sexual experiences and made salacious jokes. I always pretended I never heard anything. I was just not interested, as I was not interested in soccer, for example.

"In Africa people reach their sexual maturity earlier than in the West. That's how ignorant I was. When I was 13 or 14, I started masturbating, but only when I opened my big art book, looking ecstatically at beautiful statues such as the Venus of Milo or the David of Michelangelo. They both gave me hard-ons. What I couldn't do at that time was to associate these magnificent works of art, depicting men and women in their physical perfection, with youngsters in flesh and blood. Some of my classmates were handsome or pretty, but I just couldn't

approach them sexually. It was like there was a chasm between the paintings and the sculptures I admired and the people I frequented. I had good friends all right, and one or two girls fell in love with me. I would never respond and the remarks fell: 'Albert is really hopeless, maybe he is homosexual, after all.' It didn't even hurt me, I didn't know what they meant. Today this kind of naiveté, at least, in developed societies, would not be believable. But that is the truth. My first sexual experience was a rape. This happened during one of our forays in the beautiful volcanic region of Auvergne, in the center of France, with my father, while we lived in Italy. I was alone, going back to our hotel through the fields, after having played a game of tennis, when a handsome woman of maybe 35 saw me. 'Oh! Aren't you the son of that Italian man, staying at the Hotel X? That's where I also reside during the summer.' I acquiesced timidly since I did remember her face. Before I knew what was going on, I found myself lying on the field, with my pants off. 'What are you doing?' I asked her, stupidly. 'Oh come on, don't tell me you're a virgin!'

As I was resisting her, she rebuked me: 'So, you prefer men!' I was so frozen and dumbfounded, that I let her rape me! And the following days, she sometimes managed to be alone with me in the hotel elevator and dragged me to her bedroom. Did I enjoy it? No, because she was a sex maniac, and everybody seemed to be aware of it—I then found out that she was the wife of a famous Parisian surgeon—especially since she would have extremely loud orgasms, and the walls were so thin that all the residents who were either resting or doing something else could hear her / us, with the damn bed and parquet creaking like hell. She later gave me a small golden heart. My father knew what she had done to me and he seemed to be proud of his son, who had now become a real man!

"I really did fall in love with my first wife, who was on the contrary, quiet and reserved. We made love in a very natural way. By that I mean, I was considerate and our love-making was exactly what the phrase means: I did it out of love mainly. I didn't know anything about foreplay, erotic games, 'blue' books, etc. In hindsight, I can say that I was not, and never have been a great lover. Sex was very secondary to me, even though I knew the facts of life. Until very late in my adult life, and after having sired two wonderful children, I wasn't even interested in other sexual practices or, for that matter, in pornography. Homosexuality was still like a cloud in my mind. I was aware of its existence but it meant nothing to me, not out of fear—don't forget that I frequented Catholic schools in Africa, during 9 years, where I heard time and

again that the sin of flesh could lead you to hell—I just never had any guilt feelings concerning sex. Which is strange, since I knew so little about it.

"My second wife was the opposite of the first one, but still I didn't change, she was the 'leader' in sexual matters and otherwise. We divorced because of our increasing incompatibility, and not for any other reasons, as some people perhaps might believe.

"I was already 38, for crying out loud, when I discovered that I liked men, especially after having met the person who is now my life partner. Yes, I suddenly woke up and began to frequent sauna baths, out of spite and distress, during the period B. left me. I became a voyeur, doing very little myself with other men, some of whom were gorgeous. I was fervently approached many a time, but I always retracted. Yes, I now enjoyed watching porn films in a cubicle and it excited me, with all these hunks sitting by my side and a few trying to stroke me—I let them do just that.

"Voilà: what a sexual nerd I was! So what am I, a hetero, a homo, a bisexual? I don't care what people call me. Now I like sex, but am not active at all. I prefer gentleness and tenderness to hard sex. But why not associate the two, with love as the main condition?

"As you can see, I always felt apart from 'the norm'! And even before I knew about sexual differences, I never liked people who despised or laughed at those who were not like them. Does that make me a militant?

"In literature, I guess so, but not in the streets. I don't demonstrate with hundreds of people; though I like Gay pride parades and have a certain admiration for drag queens and all the colorful characters who insist upon marking their differences conspicuously. I believe they are very courageous and that we need such people to confront the petit-bourgeois' hypocritical and inane attitude, inasmuch as there have always been, among the Popes, the Monsignors and the priests, what they themselves call sexual perverts. They are the sinners, not the other way round—didn't Jesus 'protect' Mary Magdalene the 'slut', against her enemies? —and it is because of the all the bunk, the nonsensical and harmful religious laws that this stupid sin became and still is the norm in every day life. 'Pope Francis, as kind as you are, you have no place in our societies, much less among the poor folk of Africa and elsewhere! It is criminal to demand that they abstain from having sexual relations or not to wear condoms! Who do you think helped to increase in huge numbers those affected by AIDS, if not

Pope John XXII, and those before him, the majority, in the world, being women, not gay people?' In Islamic countries, it is even much worse, but let's not go into that."

⎯◌◌⎯

GETTING PERSONAL: DIGGING EVEN DEEPER

Well, dear Readers, I cannot be absolutely certain, but I do feel that I can press a bit further now. And so I ask: "What experiences, Albert, can possibly be related to the pedophilia scene?" And here is his answer:

"When I was 7, in Elisabethville / Lubumbashi (DR Congo), I was raped by a nephew of my father, who must have been about 13. Of course I didn't understand why he asked me to undress and to submit myself to his lust, lest I be 'denounced'. He used me quite a few times and I obliged, scared of the promised punishment if I didn't, yet feeling intuitively that what he was doing to me was wrong.

"Much later, during my second stay in NYC, I was already an adult of 32, and I had been married to my daughter's mother, and divorced, I still didn't have any homosexual inclinations, in spite of the fact that I frequented artists and gay people in Greenwich Village.

"I received, via my Belgian publisher, Pierre Deméyère, a letter from a bishop who had read 'Eclats de Malachite' and who had lauded the book so fervently that he invited me to stay at the 'Collège' (equivalent to high-school, not to the American College) in Namur, Wallonia (southern Belgium), of which he was the Principal, when I returned to Europe during the summer vacation, (I flew across the Atlantic every year, to rejoin my family in Italy), for a couple of weeks, just before the Summer recess. My parents and I believed it was an honor that I ought to accept.

"Of course, I was still so naive in matters of sexual differences and orientations (again I knew they existed, as I knew that hunters were hacking to death baby seals in Canada, and I did feel for people who were victims of

50

homophobia and for all the other innocent people who acted differently to the norm in general, suffering from injustices of all kinds; in other words, I was always on their side). Yes, at the ripe age of 32, for crying out loud, I was still incredibly ignorant, to the point that I didn't understand why people of the same sex would make advances to me. I would refuse politely and with such equanimity, never getting mad, that these young men thought I might be, well, retarded.

"I thus took the plane from Milan to Brussels, then a train to Namur, where the bishop was waiting for me at the station. He was ever so kind, and kept on saying what a sensitive writer I was. Imagine how flattered I felt, coming from the Principal of Namur's best-known 'Collège'. After accompanying me to his private suite—yes, he invited me to stay in the guest-room of the school's most privileged apartment—and he showed me around the premises; then we toured the town, which is one of Belgium's loveliest, set on a cliff, at the confluence of the rivers Meuse and Sambre. Namur is the capital city of Wallonia (the French-speaking part of the country) and is known for its Citadel, a medieval fortress with beautiful gardens. It also harbors the Felicien Rops Museum, with the work of the artist, who created scandal after scandal because of his erotic and pornographic paintings and drawings. We did not visit the museum, of course. Now I have in my library a magnificent book with the complete art works of Felicien Rops. He is still deemed, nowadays—we're in 2017!—a filthy pornographer by the petit-bourgeois and the fundamentalists of all stripes.

"We dined with hundreds of students at the Collège's mess hall. The food was abundant and quite tasty, considering we were in a school. He introduced me to them as a very promising writer who was studying in the United States. As I said before, I had my own room and my own shower and WC, a real luxury. I slept quite well that first night and woke up with a puzzled feeling. The bishop was sitting on the edge of my bed, stroking my face. He said nothing and went down through the lower opening of my pyjamas, then started caressing my penis. I got a hard-on but was taken aback, bamboozled, for I never expected something like that, coming, what's more, from such a respected personality.

"It was the first time in my life that I became conscious that a person of the same sex wanted to make love to me. By the way, the rape committed by my cousin when I was seven got 'diluted' in the marshes of my memory—yes there was a total blank and it never traumatized me, for I had so many other real problems as a child.

51

"I was so dumbstruck by the bishop's temerity that I let him touch me without reacting. He even introduced a finger into my anus. Then, without so much as a murmur, he presented me with his penis. It was so big—I had never seen one of such a size, even in the marble statues I admired so much—that I gagged. He thrust it in front of my mouth. I didn't know why but I instinctively clenched my teeth. Then he told me to lie on my stomach, and said that he wouldn't hurt me. There, I got the fright of my life, for his knob was as large as a ping pong ball and his testicles were twice as large as mine. I did what he had asked, but the moment when his knob touched my buttocks, I shivered and had the courage to say: 'No, please, nooo.' And he stopped. But every day thereafter, he came to bid me good night, stroking my penis and asking me to do the same to his, and I complied, yet I always felt strange and uneasy. He had that kind of sweet talk that didn't allow you—at least me—to reject him brutally.

"Again, that extraordinary experience did not traumatize me or make me want to explore the world of homosexuality. Remember, I got married a second time to my son's mother. This exploration came about after I had divorced her, reaching now the age of ... 43."

Whoah! Okay ... back to analysis of the novel. This great novel is not only about personal identity crises, but also about the dilemmas of fighting against patterns of thinking and behavior ... about the human archetype in general. Much like the ancient Greeks, Russo writes about the inevitability of failure in resisting one's inherited psychology; and assuming the consequences of one's "lot in life" as if they are the result of social and psychological genetics and addictions. Even at the end of the story—in spite of a rigorous Christian re-education—the protagonist in this story returns to her psychological genetic roots, and attempts to once again make things "right" by adopting a child and re-naming it after her mulatto lover. There are perhaps many persons who see having a child and giving it a new and better life as a way to re-create their own pasts. But by naming/re-naming the child as a symbol of one's difficult past the resistance to letting go and moving forward is perhaps self-sabotaged.

The writing is engaging and convincing, as is the story and its development ... but I personally want Léodine to break free of her chains of slavery (which she has herself reinforced, albeit perhaps unwittingly). And yet, the believability of the story lies not only in the excellent writing, but also in the understanding that it could not have developed and ended in any other way. I am left sated ... but on another level still dissatisfied; not with the story or the writing, but with the confirmation that the human race and personal history are doomed to repeat themselves.

This is a novel with a classic foundation of ideas and development. It is—in retrospect—perhaps predictable, just as human development and behavior is perhaps "predictable" to palm-readers or psychics. (Eg. by observing another's personality traits, attitudes and behavior patterns it is not difficult to gauge what will happen in the near or not-so-distant future.) But the power and success of this novel lies—in fact—in its predictability, and in the literary skills employed to build up the story detail far beyond that of the classic Greek myths.

ON PRINCES AND GODS, AND EUR-AFRICAN EXILES

In "Princes and Gods" and "Eur-African Exiles" Albert Russo achieves new heights in his mastery of storytelling. "Princes and Gods" is fast-paced and, despite the relative simplicity of the writing style, he weaves an intricate mélange of stories within stories which—although they may at times seem to be asides or even distractions—ultimately all fall into place as the culmination of the storyline reveals itself in a beautiful and wild fashion that reflects and illustrates the uselessness of resisting the inevitable ... be it change in interpersonal relationships or politics. In Russo's account of Burundi's movement towards independence, local affairs are never fully extricable from influences and pressures from the outside world, be they from neighboring Congo, or from politics, cultural pressures and interference from Europe, the US, Russia or China. The novel perhaps aptly describes the mirrored effects of inertia and change that reverberate and are mirrored on all levels, from love relationships and friendships to pressures for political and institutional changes. And yet, in this novel Russo again manages to acquaint the reader with the mentality of intrinsic African justice, and the necessity of achieving eventual balance when infringements and transgressions have taken place.

In this work the author employs verse, ancient folklore, historical and political facts and interpretations, as well as richly detailed descriptions of people, places, and environments in order to transport the reader to Burundi at a particular interval in history in its transition from colonial to independent status. Russo thus "occupies" the readers' minds in a complicated chess-like game until the real purpose of the build-up rears its head in the final pages and results in a "feu d'artifice" unimagined in the beginning or middle sections of the book. And, true in spirit to Russo's Africa, in the end there is no European "true believer, or nationalist" who wins—but rather a taming of passion to a sense of order more in synch with the soul of Africa.

In "About Princes and Gods", an essay by Jean-Luc Breton, published in Small Press Review and World Literature Today, Breton writes: "Albert Russo raises then the ultimate question of the effect of colonialism, a political system in which humaneness (love, tolerance and delight in natural beauty) is eventually dissolved into the disheartening racial equality of greed, contempt and murder."

Albert Russo has made the following synopsis of "Eur-African Exiles" on the back cover of the book: "This is the story of Sandro Romano-Livi, a young Italian Jew, leaving his Mediterranean island by boat, for the Belgian Congo (DR Congo), in 1926, as a stowaway. Of his adventurous life in Central Africa, during the first fifteen years, of David-Kanza (aka Daviko), the mulatto son he adopts, a secret he will disclose to his white Anglican fiancée, Gloria Simpson, born and raised in Rhodesia (Zimbabwe). Of their two daughters, Astrid and Dalia. Of his family's difficult situation and of their hopes. Of the loss of his parents and baby sister, who were sent to a Nazi concentration camp. Of his many travels in the African bush and of his ultimate success as a businessman. Of the family's departure to northern Italy, where they will settle, just before Central

Africa's tragic events, whilst Sandro and Daviko will remain in Africa for a longer period. Of their love of the black continent and their incurable nostalgia. Of Astrid's later humanitarian activities in Botswana and Malawi."

In my own foreword to this book I wrote:

"This is a controversial book ... not especially in regards to the story itself, which is interesting, endearing and entertaining. It is controversial in its usage of a simple narrative writing style infused throughout with commentary that is highly socio-political in nature. The novel is both propaganda in literature and literary propaganda. Mr. Russo effectively lays out his tale in such a matter-of-fact fashion that the reader eagerly devours facts, fiction and political commentaries by the author without so much as blinking an eye. And Mr. Russo accomplishes this without railroading the reader into the absurd (as in the case of «Candide» by Francois-Marie Arouet Voltaire).

Moreover, this is a «feel good» book. Even atrocities are given no more weight than personal pleasures and misfortunes. This because—from the narrator's perspective – the reality of the here and now in Africa is always the central point of focus. As a result, the reader is led through a cinematic voyage—sometimes by boat, sometimes by train, and sometimes by car—through a myriad of literary landscapes, rich images and experiences of Life, which feel at once timeless, ever-changing and as natural as the magic of Africa itself."

And I stand by those lofty words, even today. I had read all of these four African novels previously, but never before as now—one after the other, and with the larger perspective achieved after having read several of Monsieur Russo's publications from the past many years. I now feel inclined to go a few steps deeper—beyond praise of his literary storytelling skills, and into the politics behind his opinions that are voiced as asides, rhetorical discourses and short justifications in his novels and poetry. Albert Russo is, in my experience, a chameleon: he is easy to notice, but difficult to know with one glance. He is himself an African diamond with many facets, and it is often in the nuances (here literary) that one can finally get a good glimpse of who the author is as a creator—in his writing and art, and as a humanist and citizen of the planet Earth.

—◦◦◦—

THE AFRICAN NOVELS: MY FINAL QUESTIONS TO ALBERT RUSSO, AND HIS RESPONSES.

Here are my final questions to Albert Russo regarding his African novels:

- Things Fall Apart, the acclaimed novel published by Nigerian author Chinua Achebe in 1958, is considered by some to be the archetypal modern African novel (written in English). Has this, or have any other post-colonial African novels, influenced your own "African Quatuor"? And if so, then how? Do you think that there is a school or specific genre associated with modern African literature? Please explain.

"Ever since I left Africa, I kept reading novels written by African-Americans and by 'new' African authors—new in the sense, that they were beginning to be discovered—such as Wole Soyinka, Chinua Achebe, Buchi Emecheta, Ngugi wa Thiong'o, Tierno Monenembo, In Koli Jean Bofane, who wrote a fabulous book set in Kinshasa, Charles Djungu Simba, who has become a close friend and who is teaching some of my own books at the University of Lubumbashi, V.Y. Mudimbe, who I believe teaches in the USA, Sony Labou Tansi, etc, in both English and French, their 'chosen' literary language. Not to mention Nadine Gordimer, JM Coetzee, Breyten Breytenbach, and Alan Paton, the author of 'Cry the Beloved country', plus many more. Here I'd like to add Doris Lessing who wrote the magnificent collection 'African stories', about her life in Rhodesia / Zimbabwe. My beloved mother and she were in the same girl school in the capital Salisbury (now Harare). They used to greet each other but remained mere acquaintances. As you probably know, Lessing became a communist, then, abandoning that ideology, she wrote many of her later books as a staunch feminist. Then too I read avidly, in France, excellent North African writers; too many to be listed here, with some of my favorites being Yasmina Khadra (a man, in spite of his feminine name), Malika Mokeddem,

56

Kateb Yacine, Azouz Begag and, especially, Assia Djebar; all of whom I met and sympathized with, and the latter became a close friend of mine—I met her in the USA when she got the prestigious Neustadt Prize for Literature (I was a member of that jury), often leading to the Nobel Prize, she was also one of the very few women sitting at the Académie Française—unfortunately, she died in 2015. All these writers have had a cumulative influence on my own work. They are too diverse to form a 'trend' or a 'school'. That suits my own eclecticism."

- You have alluded to some of your views regarding international interference, slave trade (both Arab and European colonial), as well as the oppression and benefits of European and American influence on African countries in many of your works. Today we can read in the news that Arab slave trade continues even now. You touch upon previous African skepticism towards Arabs (due to slave trade) in your books. Could you comment briefly on your political perspectives concerning these issues, including the unfairness of post-colonial historical-political assessments of Belgian colonialism?

"Referring back to slave-trading—which has existed since Antiquity—I insist on teaching about that savage and criminal practice, in its entirety, not only tackling the European-led crime, but also that of the Muslim countries, which is still going on today, and of the African tribal chiefs too. In other words—and it isn't the first time I am saying this—history, which I deem to be a very 'volatile' and 'subjective' (meaning not scientific) field, ought to be regarded as a work-in-perpetual-progress. I respect only historians who can admit that they may be wrong, not the majority who claim that they possess the absolute truth! I, who am not a historian, believe I know much more about Belgian-ruled Africa than most of the so-called specialists. I have heard my share of untruths and biases concerning the Belgian Congo, especially coming from the Anglo-Saxons, who I repeat reflect the biases and the old clichés of the British. You will read all my thoughts on that subject in my African Quatuor. And I too have made mistakes in my own assessments, particularly when I was younger and when I believed in some of the nonsense printed under glossy covers."

- You have written in your African Quatuor that you (or at least the "speaker" in one of your novels) are skeptical towards persons who are racists towards general populations. You are both African and a "man of the world", well-traveled, you are multilingual, and you have a love of many cultures. And yet, you have expressed skepticism towards Moslem/Arab cultural practices, religion and politics in previous and current books. You also write that you do (or the characters in your novels) not feel obliged to always be "politically-correct".

a) First of all, is cultural skepticism necessarily racist, in your opinion? Do you feel any restrictions upon utilizing your freedom of speech as an author when writing about intercultural/interracial differences and conflicts? Have there been restrictions from publishers upon your freedom of speech regarding socially-sensitive issues? If so, how do you deal with these—do you re-write, omit … or find another publisher?

b) You are both African, European, a Jew of Sephardic heritage, and an avid literary advocate of human rights. I know you as a lover of mankind (all races) and an Agnostic by faith. Please explain how your own background/experiences, religious beliefs and human rights politics have influenced your skepticism towards aspects of Moslem/Arab culture, politics and practice. You write that you generally felt accepted as an African of Jewish heritage in Africa, but that Africans were skeptical to Arabs. How has that influenced your writing of these novels (and subsequent ones), and your views today?

c) In summary, do you—now, and as an Agnostic—feel that Christianity served colonial and post-colonial Congo, Burundi and Rwanda well, or was it perhaps a "mixed bag"? What were the benefits and disadvantages of Christianity at the time you lived in Africa? And how has that changed today, if at all? Russo's comments follow here:

"As you already know, I am an Agnostic and can even claim to be a Humanist. I very rarely had to change my texts concerning religious issues, except lately, when I have mentioned Islamic terrorism. I understand how dangerous it is for publishers to print some of my views, but why do they never discuss my skepticism regarding other religions, including Christianity and fundamentalists of other faiths, like the Ultra-Orthodox Jews? We do live in a world where political-correctness has become more important than freedom of expression, all this, being the result of fear... FEAR. Yes, I too am afraid of those I deem to be less than human, who are able to murder thousands of innocents of their own religion and the so-called 'Infidels'. They are despicable,

whether their skin is white, blue, black, green or even grey; and they seem to favor RED, the color of blood.

"Christians in the Belgian Congo, Rwanda and Burundi have both brought good things: thousands of priests and nuns were sincerely devoted to the well-being and to the education of Africans, both in their native tongues and in French, and by doing so, these people sacrificed their own comfort.

"The very negative side, from the beginning, was to instill fear into the souls of children and adults alike, with the so-called original and deadly sins that lead to Hell, whilst defining their ancient spirits as the work of the devil.

"But African ingenuity has all along been able to merge both their traditional Animism with modern Christianity. Unfortunately, many of the contemporary so-called Televangelists, hailing from America, have added unwanted confusion to an already fragile syncretism. Then too, the Popes have done a lot of harm to the present African population, by teaching them to be abstinent—which shows a total lack of sexual knowledge and African mores—and not to wear condoms, which is even more criminal, and which has led to an exponential increase of HIV-AIDS, making the Black Continent the major sufferer of that disease.

"Now, I see another dangerous evolution: the forced Islamization of Black African countries, as well as a multiplication of Christian sects. There are now in the DR Congo dozens of such sects and their initiators behave as if they were demigods, leading their flocks into the wrong path, because these 'new' priests are just plain crooks and they demand that the parishioners give them most of the little money they possess. All of this is quite disheartening, and whereas I respect people who have faith in their god, i.e., people who are righteous and help their neighbors, like those Christians and Muslims who hid Jews from the Nazis and the fascists during WWII, I dislike church mice, which my heroine Zapinette would call 'church rats', or even worse, 'church roaches'. There is the French equivalent, which is: 'grenouilles de bénitier'. They are terrible hypocrites, who, like the French Nazi collaborators of Vichy, are capable of doing tremendous harm.

"Remember how the 'Very Catholic' Isabel II who, with the Pope's blessing, allowed the 'Holy Inquisition' to take form and to murder non-Christians. Today there is Jean-Marie Le Pen, in France, who claims to be a good Catholic, while hating both Jews and Muslims alike, forgetting, willingly, that

Jesus was a Jew, a rabbi, and that the so-called Last Supper, was in fact the feasting of Pesah (which gave way to Easter).

"To conclude with this unsolvable subject, I'd like to add that Jesus was 'made' Christian by his followers decades after his death. During his lifetime he wouldn't have understood if people called him Jesus Christ (a Greek invention). Actually his original name was Yehoshua. In the very beginning, there was Judaism, then it turned into a Judeo-Christian sect, and finally into what we now know as Christianity, in the name of which Jews have been tortured, murdered, chased from country to country, for over 2000 years. In the name of whom exactly? In the name of Jesus, who would abhor and condemn such behavior. The same atrocities are now being committed by thousands of people in the name of Allah!

"And, unfortunately, dictators like Mugabe in Zimbabwe or Museveni in Uganda, both Christians, have adopted the regressive Victorian attitude of demonizing homosexuals and abortionists.

"Go tell it on the mountain!"

JAMES BALDWIN'S LETTER TO ALBERT RUSSO.

Dear Albert Russo:

I am sorry to have taken so long to answer you, but l have been busy, and a trifle ill—actually, I think more exhausted than ill but doctors can be very boring. Anyway, I'm back at the typewriter.

I've read everything you sent me, and I like your work very much indeed. It has a very gentle surface and a savage under-tow—the fiction—and I applaud the wicked portrait of Ionesco. You're a dangerous man.

I don't doubt the general publishing reaction to your work. You are saying something, after all, which no one particularly wants to hear and saying it, furthermore, from a particularly intimidating point of view.

With your permission, however, I might send the excerpts you have sent me on to a friend of mine, at Random House, in New York. My friend is the Black woman novelist, Toni Morrison, who is an editor there. She is, in every way, beautiful, extraordinary, swift, and knows what you are talking about. Or you can send whatever you want, using my name, and I'll warn her to expect to hear from you.

Let me know how you want to handle it, and we'll see what happens. You might wish to send a broader collection.

I'm in Paris on the 24th of this month and hope to see you.

All the best,

James Baldwin.

PART TWO

POETRY WAS HIS FIRST LOVE

ALTHOUGH I KNOW MUCH OF HIS WORK RATHER WELL, ALBERT RUSSO never ceases to surprise and impress me. He is very competent as a novelist, and equally so—if not even more—as a poet, short story writer, essayist and photographer. In this section I will address his poetry, and then his short stories.

No matter what the genre, Albert Russo is a master storyteller; and his poems, short stories and novellas are—in fact—often stories of varying lengths. While his novels are usually quite detailed in their descriptive qualities, even his shortest poems (yes, even his haiku poems) manage to transport the reader into the intended mindset of the author, even if only telling about a few moments in a larger story in one history of the species of Man. I say this because Albert's work always has a sense of universality about it, no matter if he uses the first or third person to tell his story; and the stories—although often alluding to a certain time or space in history—somehow echo the repetitiveness of human thought and behavior, throughout the ages.

The versatility he demonstrates across genres and styles of writing is—indeed—unusual, as not all authors manage to master several. Writing novels is quite a different process, and requires different approaches and skills than more condensed genres, such as short stories and poetry. The shorter the form, the more important it is to find the correct words, rhythms and multiple-layered meanings within the smaller framework. Even if writing from the context of a single thought within a moment in time, the writer must have an understanding of the greater context (the larger story) as well. In this way, poetry is written first in the mind ... and then condensed and expanded in written form. I include "expanded" because a successful poem can perhaps be likened to skipping a small rock across a pond—creating ripples and reverberations which both reflect the greater omnipotence of the water and temporarily alter its periphery and identity. And there we have that word again: identity. Also in his poetry, short stories and novellas Russo explores identity in all of its expressions and forms, and in various languages and styles.

ALBERT RUSSO'S POETRY COLLECTION: CROWDED WORLD OF SOLITUDE, VOLUME 2

In the book's preface, Leigh Eduardo writes:

"His work reaches into the very soul of contemporary living. Here, one comes to grips with many contemporary problems, all beautifully crafted and possessing the Russo hallmark of subtle observation. Each poem is a gem in its own right."

Those words by Leigh Eduardo perfectly describe the intentions and accomplishments of Albert Russo in this splendid edition of poems. I will comment on his longer prose poems a bit later in this section but first, Mr. Russo has included many linked haiku poems in this volume—and so many that I believe that they warrant special consideration. Here are some selected examples that typify Albert Russo's haiku.

HAIKU FOR THE SOUL

look at your fingers

how complex its geography

so much history

when you close your eyes

shooting stars crisscross the dais

your afterlife unfolds

to see the light within

the sun must set all around

night flowers open up
laughter masks great pains
smiles are the masks of laughter
then there are cries of joy
little does man care
about animals' feelings
nature takes revenge
the death of corals
presages the end of mankind
we use them as jewels
if books disappear
forests might be saved
but we will lose our soul

—ww—

HAIKU PLEAS TO A CONCUBINE

being swallowed live
is what i feel when you scream
so please let me breathe
ranting against fate
will not do you any good
you are bound to die
why did you kick me?
our hearts have dried long ago
bleeding makes a mess
switch off the bed lamp

aren't you tired of seeing me?
you'll be my nightmare
god bless daytime thoughts
that's the only time you are dead
virtual solace
remember how we met
you were looking for your dog
and i for a friend
o, to be lonely
and to fight with one's shadows
instead of with you

———⊶⊷———

HAIKU INFLORESCENCE

deadly nightshades
berries glowing like ripe boils
a witch's delight
spike of spring bells
honey-tinted flowers
hailing an angel
a dragonfly
brushes past a spiderwort
dreams in deep blue
hydrangeas stand guard
around a cluster of roses
baroque symphony

a splash of purple

busy-lizzy from Zanzibar

impatient, hot-blooded

a hermaphrodite

friend to epileptics

poisonous mistletoe

rugged and fragrant

when everything else wilts

count on the rock cress

brandy bottles

feathery water lilies

pungent roquefort smell

slipper orchid

aphrodite's favorite

suave and sensual

—⚭—

As noted before, Albert Russo is a great storyteller—even in his short literary works such as haiku and longer prose poems. He is also a poet who puts his own personal spin on well-known literary styles, ranging from narrative prose poetry to lyrical haiku art. Russo's love for haiku is not surprising. A man with so many thoughts, and who uses such an extensive palette of words in his novels, also knows the importance and value of both understanding and practicing the power of written words at all levels, and in all literary forms. Haiku often lends a "sharpness" to the mind—challenging both the right and left sides of the brain to interact with the workings of the emotional body. But, of course, Russo did not invent modern haiku. Haiku art has gone through some revolutionary changes in its development. It is perhaps not really possible to understand any form of new expression—literary, or otherwise—without some basic understanding of the history of what has been before, and the need for new movement, new directions, new language, new concepts … and, sometimes, even, radical change. Therefore, I will briefly trace the historical developments of Japanese poetry and haiku; and then take a closer look at Albert Russo's own modern haiku.

—◌◌◌—

A SHORT HISTORICAL SYNOPSIS—
THE EARLY ROOTS OF SHORT JAPANESE LYRICAL
POETRY

In its traditional form the haiku has existed for almost five hundred years. However, its roots stretch back to the Heian period of Japan (seventh century to eleventh century); and originally in the form of "uta" (short and lyrical poems/songs) which comprised part of pre-Buddhist or early Shinto rituals. These poems were inspired by various celebrations, prayers and eulogies, courting, planting and harvesting. The most practiced and recognized of these poetic forms—the "waka"—was characterized by 31 phonetic units ("on") which were broken into five lines with a 5-7-5-7-7 count. Waka quickly gained in popularity, and the most proficient writers gained considerable notoriety. From the ninth century it further developed into what is today known as "tanka" which is characterized by three lines with 5-7-5 syllable counts followed by two lines of seven syllables. These short lyrical poems gained preference over longer poetry forms ("choka").

The popularity of writing and reciting short verse spread to all socio-economic levels of Japanese society once linking of verses became a popular pastime, in the forms of "renga" (linked verse) and "kusari-no-renga" (linked verse in chains). The popularity of poetry amongst the lower classes in the mid-sixteenth century prompted a renaissance whereby less rigid forms gave way to lighter ones ("haikai", or "renka"). Characteristic of "haikai" was an initial three lines ("hokku"), which had to include a seasonal word ("kireji") as well as a "cutting/exclamatory" word. The first three lines of the "hokku" were of utmost importance.

Towards the end of the seventh century a poet named Bashō (the pen name of Matsuo Chūemon Munefusa, born 1644, in Iga province, Japan—died November 28, 1694, Osaka, Japan), developed his own style by simplifying the form to consist solely of the "hokku" (the main three initial lines). This became known as the "haiku". Bashō is known for other aesthetic and conceptual changes such as promotion of "karumi" (lightness) and spontaneity. Lucien Stryk wrote in "On Love and Barley: Haiku of Bashō", Penguin, 1985:

"Bashō's mature haiku style, Shofu, is known not only for karma, but also for two other Zen-inspired aesthetic ideas: sabi and wabi. Sabi implies contented solitariness, and in Zen is associated with early monastic experience, when a high degree of detachment is cultivated. Wabi can be described as the spirit of poverty, an appreciation of the commonplace, and is perhaps most fully achieved in the tea ceremony, which, from the simple utensils used in the preparation of the tea to the very structure of the tea hut, honours the humble."

While the haiku has undergone many changes since that time, today's haiku still has remarkable similarities to the form developed by Bashō. Other notable haiku poets who worked in the tradition of Bashō included Buson (Yosa Buson, original surname Taniguchi, born 1716 in Kema, Settsu province, Japan—died Jan. 17, 1784, Kyōto) and Issa (Kobayashi Issa, born 1763 in Shinano province, Japan—died Jan. 5, 1828), as well as the rebellious Shiki (Masaoka Shiki, born as Masaoka Noboru on October 14, 1867, Onsen District, Ehime province, Japan—died Sept. 19, 1902, Tokyo, Japan). While Bashō was a "wandering poet" and is known for his travel "diaries", Buson (like Bashō) was little concerned with the great universal questions and delighted in painting colourful pictures and (sometimes) the simple state of loneliness; and Issa is to some referred to as both a poet of fate and a poet of the mundane—often resulting in a sense of cathartic personal engagement ... whereas Shiki (the literary theoretician and haiku innovator) is known for his introspective realism ... and he is also known for his criticism of Bashō (and his insistence that it was Buson, not Bashō, who was the greatest haiku poet of all time).

THE CHARACTERISTICS OF
TRADITIONAL HAIKU TODAY

As with all art forms, haiku art explores personal expression through a lens of subjectivity vs. concreteness, and within a framework of genre characteristics, practices and accepted formats. Through the course of time, various trends and approaches may be subject to new ideas, if not major innovations. In classical music, centuries-old practices and the composers' notational directions—as well as historical ways of approaching older musical forms—provide guidelines which must be adhered to for accepted interpretation and performance. And yet, every now and then, an accomplished performer—perhaps a pianist, a violinist or another composer—may add his/her own "personal touch" through inter-pretational freedoms not generally associated with the classical ways of performing the work(s) in question. Some are considered to be interesting and successful, while many others are not. It is not always clear what a particular artist can expect to "get away with" (i.e. gain audience/reader acceptance for) at any particular time in history, or why. And it is not unusual to hear "critics" or "experts" dismiss innovations as improper as regards style, or possibly because "it just does not work for me"; and the most conservative (or, if you permit, the rather judgmental expression "closed minded") are often those persons who know a bit about classical art forms and history but who are not themselves accomplished or self-secure enough to understand the possibilities and expansiveness of art beyond "the restraints of traditional guidelines", or who may be otherwise threatened by experimentation and change. Art is a powerful medium—and new ideas expressed and presented through art are both celebrated and feared, by academics, non-academics, the wealthy, the not-so-rich, the politically-powerful and those who would question their power.

Haiku—originally an art form whose successes were attributed to and enjoyed by a small elite—has been "socially-decentralized" over recent centuries, in both appreciation and practice—not only in Japan, but in other countries as well. Today, haiku is still enjoyed both as entertainment and as "high-art" (and often even as a first approach to art and poetry-writing for the "common man and woman"; and novices), but there also remain those who—for whatever reasons—would emphasize tradition over artistic new-development. Is it not possible to embrace and allow for both; and to have perhaps two thoughts in one's mind at the same time? Is critical assessment of "good vs. not-so-good" haiku strictly determined through adherence to guidelines associated with traditional practices, or do the most accomplished haiku artists possess an extraordinary insight and vision which permits them to bend, expand upon and give new life to traditions—perhaps even while challenging technical limitations and "truths"? And is not re-invention and re-interpretation of art a necessity for the very survival of the various art forms—in order to maintain relevance in a changing world that is subject to fast-paced developments influenced by technological advances and globalization, as well as changes in political-cultural perspectives, and linguistics? Well, haiku has not only survived and evolved, but it has developed worldwide into a mainstream art form that is far more than a Japanese curiosity. And yet, achievement of true mastery of this art form today is dependent upon the same combinations of genius, technique and expanded vision as in other great accomplishments in art, philosophy and science. Verily, the art of haiku—like abstract painting—is dependent upon both planning and spontaneity, an understanding of internal rhythm and dynamics, and communicating an overall feeling of lightness and ease, in ways that are different from large paintings and larger genres within prose-writing. Reductionism in art demands the ability to not only synthesize ideas into smaller canvases, but also to express and intimate artistic and philosophical expansionism well beyond minimalism—often employing simplicity and introspection to approach complexities.

Let us take a look at these generally-accepted characteristics of traditional haiku today—in Japan, and outside of Japan. Haiku are often "reflections" expressed through a single moment, but encompassing much more. Traditionally, Japanese haiku employs reflections on nature, or the seasons (time of year). The Japanese language is particularly rich as regards the number of "Kigo", or "season words" available, but these are very often implied rather than expressed in a strongly-overt manner. By avoiding writing narratives in the first-person as well as similes, metaphors etc., then the focus upon the universality of the specific moment is by many perceived as more effective—aided by visually-descriptive references to nature—and often leads to a better-written traditional haiku. Other universal "guidelines" to successful haiku-writing often include writing about a particular place, writing in the immediate present, showing action/activity rather than describing one's feelings about it with adjectives, avoiding employing needless or redundant words, and avoiding obvious rhyme. While most contemporary haiku artists and "experts" would resist the notion of "rules and regulations" in haiku-writing, there do exist guidelines which are widely accepted. Haiku form in classical Japanese haiku is generally based upon a system of employing seventeen "on" (or sounds) which follow a 5-7-5 pattern over three lines. The Japanese language is perhaps more inclined towards expression with 5-7 rhythms than other languages (as in English), in which this is not as "natural" or free-flowing. As a result, haiku-writing in some non-Japanese languages allows for less syllables than the seventeen "on-based" haiku. Nevertheless, many non-Japanese haiku artists often still adhere to using seventeen "syllables" in their haiku. For them, achieving a simplistic and natural flow can become complicated purely because of differences in language structures and rhythmic patterns. These challenges can, in turn, also make it difficult to achieve another Japanese tradition in haiku-writing: to limit the "cutting" (the number of real "breaks" or pauses) to just once in an otherwise natural and unrestricted flow or words and meaning, and generally at the end of either the first or second line of the haiku (often expressed in English with a long dash or a colon).

ON ALBERT RUSSO'S HAIKU

Here Albert Russo evokes sentiment that howls from his spleen—
sometimes an elegiac lamentation crying out for a better and more
reasonable world, and at other times a voice despairing over
loneliness and the difficulties of communication and love
relationships. And then there are haiku poems that sparkle—like
dewdrops in the sunlight—and merely allow the reader to dive into
the magic that he creates with his beautifully descriptive imagery, as
in HAIKU INFLORESCENCE. These small works are truly well-
polished gems that have retained their spontaneity and freshness.
Through his creation of a narrative form through linked verse, there
is a wonderful lyrical quality that is occasionally mumbling or
humming to oneself, and that—at other times—sings out with a full
voice. There are also hints of stream of consciousness-writing, adding
an extra layer of introspection, which make for a magical journey
inside oneself.

Russo's haiku poetry mostly adheres to the traditional 5-7-5
format but clearly breaks away from many of the above-mentioned,
perhaps somewhat restrictive, guidelines which typify classical haiku.
For him, the infamous "haiku moment" is more-or-less non-existent,
as he extends the "moment" to include the poem in its entirety. In
addition, Mr. Russo's subject matter and themes mirror those of his
novels, short stories and novellas in that they directly link personal
introspection with questions of a universal nature—be they of
human relationships, political or social ideologies etc. He manages to
achieve an "internal rhythm" in his haiku that extends the pulse
from stanza to stanza but yet allows the reader to appreciate each
individual haiku as a poem in its own right. Nature plays a role in
his haiku—just as in his descriptive longer texts—but that role is
more descriptive rather than essential to haiku interpretation. Is
Albert Russo's haiku style modern? Yes. Is it innovative? Again, yes.
Is it revolutionary? Perhaps not, as non-Japanese haiku art has
advanced and developed significantly over recent decades, and surely
Albert Russo has been influenced by this "artistic liberation".
However, his general adherence to the 5-7-5 format in English-

language haiku suggests that Mr. Russo preferred to find alternative ways to break those "rules"—rather choosing to extend the traditional practice of employing seventeen syllables into a larger presentation of linked haiku where several of the haiku work together to express a more complicated and descriptive "moment". I have posed several questions to Mr. Russo regarding his haiku style, his love of haiku, the role and function of haiku in his literary process etc.

INTERVIEW QUESTIONS TO ALBERT RUSSO
REGARDING HIS HAIKU-WRITING

Poetry was your first love, and you often seem to desire to challenge yourself with complicated or difficult themes and style experimentations within various literary genres. Do you, yourself, see a link between your haiku-style and that of your larger prose? What is the role and function of haiku in your literary process? While it is clear that you are poetic in your longer and shorter prose, I would ask you whether (or not) you consider your approach to novels, novellas and short stories to be that of a poet, or if you (perhaps) assume a different writer frame of mind / identity (if you will) when you write poetry? How do you "break down" these stories/narratives into short poetry? Do you go into an intuitive "literary trance" while thinking about a larger theme and then accentuate the various thoughts/elements into linked haiku, or is the process entirely planned? What is your background and relationship to haiku-writing ... have you studied traditional Japanese haiku, and have you been influenced by recent developments in contemporary Western haiku? You sometimes efficiently create abstractions in your short poetry through usage of various descriptive details which you pit against one another, resulting in multi-layered complexity. In your longer, narrative literary works you stretch these abstractions out over several paragraphs/pages. Does the "speeding up" of time to tell your story in haiku give you extra excitement in terms of finding the word combinations and associations that give the most appropriate meanings on various levels of comprehension? What is it about haiku-writing that you love so much?

And here is his response:

"As far as haiku is concerned, I experimented with the style by chance and I enjoyed it so much that it became a natural addition to my more 'conventional' poetry. With haiku, I feel free to tackle any subject, on the spot, without much reflection, which is not the case with my 'regular' poems. That is now what I write more easily when I'm waiting for my turn at a doctor's office or at the bank—here in Israel, and I appreciate that system, you always take a ticket and have a seat, until your number is called. When the queue is long, you can wait up to half an hour or more, quietly, for unlike what I knew in France, nobody here pushes or shoves. Also, with haiku I am capable of writing humor, or even nonsense, of which I later on try to make some sense. Blessed be Matsuo Bashō for inventing it. I even once wrote a whole sequence of haiku—three pages long—about the foods that I favor, from all corners of the world. Something I never thought of doing before. Sometimes I even try to play with geometric or figurative forms, assembling verses in pyramidal and other shapes, such as a question mark or a balloon. I also write some Tanka, but seldom."

ALBERT RUSSO'S PROSE POETRY IN CROWDED WORLD OF SOLITUDE, VOLUME 2

Albert Russo's prose poetry (in both Crowded World of Solitude, Volume 2 and Gaytude) are rich in narratives, descriptive imagery and his ideologies/socio-political ideas. Here I will first present some of his prose poems from Crowded World of Solitude, Volume 2 and from Gaytude, and then give more commentary.

RELENTLESSLY YOURS

so taken, you don't even have time

for your own business

more often than not

you're just busy being busy

it's all that incessant busyness

that makes you dizzy

and time flies

but you're too busy to notice

and when you do realize

it's late, oh so very late

and you wished you had

more than one lifetime

for never has time

seemed so pressed, so precious

not yours, everyone else's

or so it appears

yet they all complain

about the same thing

and their echo buzzes

in your ears

amidst it all

you hear someone whisper

I'm going to die

and someone else reply

sorry, all the lines are busy
a moment later:
I am dead
me too, says the other voice
they both were
in no time
what the latter did not realize
being far too busy to listen
was that the former
had come to fetch him
from the other world

ANIMA

when something dies
a little in us dies too
'tis writ in the memory
of our genes
but the mind forgets
so that when a flower withers
it no longer wrenches any tears
a sunburnt cactus
leaves but a shadow
in the region of our heart
how futile do artists appear
in this techno-saturated world

but they exist to remind us
that a piece of wood
can also have a soul
like the Pinocchio
of many a childhood
and while the environment
continues to bleed
man regales it
with virtual trash
confounding the imagination
to the point in which
suicide becomes a welcome relief

—m—

DRIFTING APART

all at once
the line of communication
becomes brittle
I never thought it could happen
you lament
that is because
you did not allow for the static
which has settled
between the two of you
but we were birds of a feather
you insist

what about the change of latitude
I ask, the sun's position
that baffled look on your face
and the ocean
that now separates you
the ozone incidence
have you taken these into account
her region has been plied
by the killer bees
but she's never mentioned them
their mere passage is enough
to trigger the process of mutation
remember how that once benign virus
found in Central African apes
developed into AIDS
and have you counted
the species being wiped out
every hour due to man's folly
do you still wonder
why the line of communication
between the two of you
is crackling

ONCE A POET, TWICE A NOMAD

Remember that poet of genius

who gave up his art still in his prime

because he could no longer stand artifice

of any kind, under any guise

the words had taken over his life

put so much pressure upon his emotions

tethered his nerves to such an unbearable degree

that his turmoil could only be assuaged

by a regular and immoderate intake of absinth

After having bitterly fought with his lover

that other wordsmith, Verlaine

mentor and discoverer emeritus

he simply and suddenly said merde to poetry

and fled to Africa

where he led a swashbuckling existence

drinking and whoring for all he was worth

losing any remnant of decency

how he reneged those gems with which

he had adorned la poésie française

preferring to deal in the real things

emeralds, pearls and rough diamonds

swindling his customers shamelessly

and even killing for a piece of bread

he caught a number of maladies

some of the venereal type

infecting boys and girls
who could have been his children
with his poisonous seed
his name nowadays spells beauty, passion
and sensuality: R I M B A U D
two syllables as contagious as ever

THE CROWDED WORLD OF SOLITUDE

there's a little girl in the park
fitting a new dress to her doll
she prattles and prattles
planning marvellous tomorrows
for them both
whilst an elderly lady dozes nearby
dreaming of the child she used to be
hungry and barefooted
walking for miles to fill her family's pail
with fresh water from the brook
a retriever yawns out of boredom
watching its mistress
then yelping at a passing cat
and that cat pretends not to have noticed
yet it too is looking for company
no not with that old grouch, it meows
I'll approach the little girl there

playing with her dummy

but she is so involved with her rag-doll

only a swarm of stinging bees would

divert her attention

so the cat strolls on and crosses

the path of a pigeon

fat arrogant thing, it hisses

just you wait till I scratch your neck

and you won't go hobbling around

like an automated egg

then suddenly a scream rents the atmosphere

someone at the other end of the park

has just tumbled out of a nightmare

all the people around her had been struck

with the curse of Lot's wife, turning into statues of salt

ALBERT RUSSO'S PROSE POETRY IN GAYTUDE

Albert Russo and I have collaborated on several projects, including "Gaytude: a poetic journey around the world" (Winner—The National Indie Excellence Awards, Gay/Lesbian Non-Fiction Category in 2009).

Here is my introduction to the book:

INTRODUCTION

— The first study for the man who wants to be a poet is knowledge of himself, full knowledge: he searches for his soul, he inspects it, he puts it to the test, he learns it. As soon as he has learned it, he must cultivate it! I say that one must be a seer, make oneself a seer. The poet becomes a seer through a long, formidable, and reasoned derangement of all the senses. All shapes of love, suffering, madness. He searches himself, he exhausts all poisons in himself, to keep only the quintessences. Ineffable torture where he needs all his faith, all his superhuman strength, where he becomes among all men the great patient, the great criminal, the great accursed one and the supreme Scholar! For he reaches the unknown! . . . So the poet is actually a thief of Fire!

—Arthur Rimbaud

Gaytude is a poetic study of both the universality and the diversity of gay experience—an experience of confluence whereby individual love, lust and identity are constantly in tandem and conflict with collective mores, customs, codes and trends. In a sense, we are all gay—inasmuch as we all seek the right to be different, as well as to be the same. For some, the pot of gold at the end of the rainbow is recognition and acceptance; and for others it is perhaps the excitement of covert intimacy and adventure. This book is dedicated to all gays, including those who flaunt their sexual orientation freely and those who still remain secretive or inactive due to still ongoing risks of abuse, harassment and execution. One day, men all over the world will be able to proudly quote from Catullus 16—this time with pride and loving spirit: "Pedicabo ego vos et irrumabo" (I shall bugger you, and you can blow me). —Adam Donaldson Powell

This book is so "realistic" that even some book reviewers can erroneously assume that it is non-fiction in verse form, as did one "reviewer" from a well-known US-based book readers' website. Another reviewer from France complained that many of the poems in "Gaytude" had appeared some years previously in another book. It may seem difficult for the present younger generation of gays to believe, but in 2009, when "Gaytude" was published, many Western-country gays were still looking for "confirmation" through global gayness—which the book both presents and provokes with. However, all persons and events in the book are fictional. Sorry to disappoint you guys!

Nonetheless, the book garnered acclaim when it (upon publication) was pronounced the Winner—of The National Indie Excellence Awards, Gay/Lesbian Non-Fiction Category. Some reviewer comments on "Gaytude" follow:

- The poems by Russo and Powell are marked by outsider-hood, the sense of being different from a fashionable or 'straight' mode of writing. — Dr. Santosh Kumar, Allahabad University, India

- Gaytude remains a remarkable piece of literature crossing infinite barriers and taboos to reach the ultimate poetry, the ultimate destination of mind and immortality.—Dr. Amitabh Mitra, Poet's Printery, South Africa.

The book's first review was by online reviewer "Kassa", who wrote the following:

- Gaytude is a collection of poetry that appears in English in the first half and then translated into French for the second half of the book. There is also a collection of pictures depicting homoerotic images throughout history as well as personal images of Albert Russo. The timelessness of these pictures is repeated as a theme within the elegant and often poignant poetry collected. The authors are two very accomplished writers who tackle a wide variety of subjects and themes that affect gay men with surprising depth and meaning. These topics will hit home especially for like-minded individuals but anyone with compassion will understand the beauty and heartache these issues bring to mind … Taken together this is a look into the lives of any and every gay man and the issues they deal with that create an aura of "different" around them. This celebration of gay life spans globally and encompasses all aspects proudly and openly. Gaytude is a wonderful collection by two powerful authors that have offered thoughts on timeless themes.—Rainbow Reviews

~ Selected longer prose poems from Gaytude ~

to ADRIAN DUMARAIS

born in 1961 in Kimberly, South Africa (by Albert Russo)

CHANGE OF REGIME

In this land where diamonds

were once extracted with blood,

the rainbow revolution

has swept away apartheid.

My father, a true-to-God Afrikaner,

oh so ferocious in his convictions,

was still not able to understand why

the splendid race to which he belongs,

that of the former masters,

for which his ancestors fought so hard,

became a minority in this country.

He also believed he could cure me

of that shameful "weakness" of character which,

"dishonors" the stronger sex, and

today he looks at me with eyes filled with hatred:

"I gave you everything," he then exclaims,

"and you betrayed me, not once, but three times.

You approve of this government of niggers,

then too, you dare to strut along with this Singh,

this Indian who is ten years older than you —

but in what muck do we live, pray tell me?"

yet, every day which passes, my love for Singh

becomes stronger,

and now I feel free to say, loud and clear,

here is my lover, a gesture which

a few years ago would have sent us both to prison,

and with the days that pass

my father moves just a little closer to the hell

he has been threatening me with

to MOKTAR BENIDRISS

born in 1982 in Hammamet, Tunisia (by Albert Russo)

MONDAY'S CATCH OF THE DAY

They were two Swiss and a Frenchman.

I picked them up while

they were retiring to their bungalow

a little bit before midnight,

a little bit tipsy, and wobbly.

The one had straw-colored hair

and was called Jeannot,

a name well-suited for him,

he was tall, lean, and beardless,

with a body as smooth as a baby's ass,

except for the dainty tuft

above his cock, soft as felt.

How delighted I was, for he was terribly bashful

and that he was still a virgin

could be read in the depths of his blue eyes.

Guy wasn't particularly beautiful,

but he had a lot of charm,

and a smile that could damn

the fiercest of wolves.

As for Rémy, he reminded me of

my former gym teacher,

with his harmoniously

developed muscles and

hair as long as that of Robin Hood.

I seduced him first.

To see Jeannot blush

as I buggered his friend

excited me tremendously;

I then pounced upon Guy,

the most willing of the three

and we came together

whilst Jeannot continued to ogle us,

trembling at the thought that

he might not come through the experience.

When his turn came,

his cheeks flushed violently

certain now that he could

no longer escape me,

he hijacked my penetrating glance

with his lovable sweetness.

I then probed his tongue and his ass,

and deflowered him memorably.

Jeannot was as delicious

as a tepid oyster,

just out of the sea.

---

to THE BOY WHOSE NAME I SHALL NOT MENTION

born in the same year as Reinaldo Arenas in Havana, Cuba (by Albert Russo)

You left us thirteen years ago, Reinaldo

dying of AIDS somewhere in the Bronx

but a friend, a generous soul,

took you into his care

during all those years of agony

in spite of his meager revenues,

in spite of his harassing night job

I shall forever be grateful to him

and he wasn't even your lover

No, I don't begrudge America

no matter what horrors we're told about it

—I've long ceased to believe in those lies—

but I do loathe my country's regime

and Fidel, whom so many leftists

hold in such awe

I refer especially to those

European intellectuals

whose blinding ideologies

have turned them

into criminal accomplices

they still look at him with

that sickening nostalgic grin,

paunchy imbeciles,

munching cocktail sausages

in front of their tv sets

who then go and scribble their pieces

for the so-called prestigious mags

Reinaldo, you were born poor but happy

on this beautiful island of ours,

which could have turned into a haven of justice

but instead, you grew up handsome

and far too sensitive and then,

adding to your bad luck,

you started writing poetry and novels

you even won some major literary prizes

here in Cuba

but the day you refused the lies

and the fraud

they hunted you down,

threw you into jail and tortured you

and our good old Fidel,

how magnanimous of him,

opened the prisons and the madhouses

and sent to the Gringo Enemy,

their inmates, as a poisoned gift,

you were dragged along with them

for you never concealed

your preference for men

They're so virtuous, our rulers!

I did not know you, Reinaldo,

but wherever you are, count me

as your friend,

for I too belong to

the despised caste of queers,

only, I did not have your courage

and remained in the closet.

I read that an American film director

has dedicated a movie in your honor,

yet you will not hear me say:

"better late than never!"

there is still too much rage in my heart

I shall instead pray for young Elian

whom Fidel has raised as a national icon,

hoping that he will not become a fag,

poor kid, he looks so very cute and innocent.

—⧗—

to SUKHUM VIT

born in Pattaya, Thailand in 1972 (by Albert Russo)

SELECTED CUSTOMERS

They call me Magic Fingers

or more prosaically

The Prince of Thai Massage

I've been on my own for three years now

selecting as my customers

the planet's handsomest men

I love to lay my hands

on the silky and hairless skin

of my rich compatriots

on that of young lean Singaporians

or of more mature Japanese men

I love to tease their flesh

anointing them with oil of jojoba and coconut milk

to which I add my own mixture of fragrant herbs

but those Asian folks, so smoothly built

are terribly shy, containing their impulses

as if they might lose their souls

though I can always sense the shudder

of pleasure my touch provokes in each one of them

it is probably due to their inbred sense of modesty

or rather to that very ancient taboo

that we all share on this continent

My most torrid memory involves a Danish marine

he wasn't very tall, but was chiselled like an Apollo

he had short hair with glints of gold

hypnotic green eyes

a mouth that begged to be nibbled

a down smooth as lambskin

especially around his ass cheeks

which he opened just enough so that my finger

could slip into his beautiful little hole

then I would turn him around

and gasp at the marvel thrust in my face

I have seen all kinds of cocks throughout my career

of various lengths and girths, colors and shapes

but never had I gazed at such perfection

balls plump like ripe tangerines

and that cock, that incredible cock

that only a Michelangelo could have sculpted

pointing its head towards me

with such potency, such tenderness

that I could no longer resist

he wanted to pay me for my 'divine performance'

in response, I yielded to him entirely, slavishly

so that he could plow my asshole to the full

and let his hot cum spurt inside my entrails

again and again

—⊶—

to ROGER MUIR

born in Glasgow, Scotland in 1978 (by Albert Russo)

CHAINED

if you trespass private property

if you cross the border without legal papers

if you glide on the handrail of an escalator

if you drive against the traffic flow

if you strike a match

near a pump at a gas station

if you throw conventions out of the window

you're in for big trouble, son!

not if you tread the snow barefoot, lost in the Rockies

not if you breathe in, day in and day out

the city's polluted air

not if you get run over by a motorbike

then suddenly you say ENOUGH

you want to do away

with all that atavism hampering your every move

with all the injustice rampant in the world

and which so many hang onto

in the name of morality and tradition

your back aches and so does your stomach

because of all the myriad excuses

that push you to comply, that force you

to smile when you feel like howling

Now you demand the right to

fill your lungs with pure ocean air

to make a bonfire of all the taboos

which have clogged your mind

ever since you learned to speak

to dance naked in the park, on the seafront

to go away and sail, sail to the end of the world

without being questioned by your folks

you'd like to spit in the faces of these bigots

these self-righteous nerds, these do-gooders

for whom appearance counts more

than happiness

but alas, you got caught in their tortuous games

for too long, without even realising it

and now you want to holler in the street

outside the church and in the courts:

let boys love boys

as freely as you love your kids

let girls love girls

and raise children if they wish

and for God's sake

SET ME FREE

FREEEEE

before I run amok

before I kill someone

YOU, if you stand in my way

ON RUSSO'S LONGER PROSE POETRY

Albert Russo's longer prose poetry—in both Crowded World of Solitude and Gaytude—is fascinating because he manages again and again to transport the reader very quickly into "his world" of thoughts, images and stories. It is almost like being a passenger on a metro and making up one's own stories about what one supposes other passengers' lives to be like. I would like to ask Albert Russo: "Where do all these stories come from, Albert?" But I suspect that he finds his stories in his mind, in the faces of strangers he passes on the streets, in the personalities of known and unknown persons—wherever. No one is safe from this "dangerous man"—with his sharp mind, drilling vision and ability to spin a tale out of loose threads that otherwise seem meaningless and unimportant.

As the title of Part Two of this book affirms, poetry was indeed Albert Russo's first love; and it was through his poetry that he and I first met. Several years ago (2005) I took contact with him because I was enthralled by his poetry book "Crowded World of Solitude, Volume 2", and wanted to inquire as to whether he might be interested in my writing a book review. This was to be my first book review ever, and the beginning of a wondrous collaboration between us that has spanned many book projects and years. My review of his 349-page book follows:

The Crowded World of Solitude, vol 2, The Collected Poems, reviewed by Adam Donaldson Powell

In an age where blatant shows of superiority are often considered a provocation, Albert Russo presents the ailing world of literary criticism with several challenges of mammoth proportions. His mastery of several literary genres, his indefatigable literary output, his command of several languages, his intellectual breadth, and the scope of his cultural and sub-cultural personal life experiences alone outclass the qualifications and/or capacities of many literary critics of this century.

Albert Russo is truly on the fast-track to becoming "famous" in his own lifetime, and indeed shows much courage and self-confidence in publishing such a formidable and challenging volume of collected poems non-posthumously. Perhaps even more so considering that poetry is not his only genre of acclaim. We live in an era where informed (and uninformed) critics often insist upon categorizing artists and artistic genius within a specific discipline, genre or art form; and where he/she who attempts to be too multidisciplinary is often considered to be "lightweight" or a "jack-of-all-trades". Albert Russo is an exception to all of the above-mentioned society-imposed and self-imposed restrictions, and clearly recalls a multidisciplinary usage of talent more particular to previous eras.

To publish one's collected poems to-date in such a large volume, spanning some thirty years of life experiences and literary development, is a very bold statement in itself. Such a collection of poems – like any other serious literary work – is expected to be even in quality, hopefully diverse in content and form, and appropriately polished (the degree of polish being both intentional and commensurate with the desired expression). In addition, writing a bilingual volume of collected poems further adds to the complexities of such an endeavour, giving rise to many questions and solutions regarding choice of original language versus translation, idiom, culture, visual communication etc.

Mr. Russo does not disappoint, and he does – in fact – both deliver substance, and an undaunted and relentless display of consistency in terms of excellent insight and craftsmanship. His collection of poetry, at times biting and hard-hitting, is both thought-provoking, amusing, intelligent and contemporary in style and subject matter.

This collection of poems denotes a clear and masterful demonstration of quality, breadth of content and form, political and social awareness, mastery of storytelling, a touch of the "bad boy", a combination of the highly-polished and the "intentionally-raw", and visual, musical and philosophical expressions—all indicative of the author's rich multicultural and experiential personal history. I find in his poetry the same literary achievements which characterize his novels and short stories: balance of intellectual rationalism and emotional presence, a solid command of the full palette of language(s) used, descriptive colour, clarity, intentional usage of abstractions, entertainment and theatrical/performance value, humour and occasional irony, and an overall sense of when to use poetic economy versus poetic rapture. Mr. Russo's poetry proclaims an almost haunting sense of musicality and visual portrayal on a subjective level. Most importantly, I find that his poetry has the power of arousing within the reader a sense of personal identification, emotion and engagement – evoking a "pas de deux between author and reader", all the while challenging the "poet" in the reader.

The poems in Crowded World of Solitude, Volume 2 are collected, and are not presented in chronological order. In fact, Mr. Russo never dated any of these works, and possibly never gave a thought to an eventual edition of his collected poems at the time of their writing. That suggests to me that poetry-writing to him has perhaps been a meditation, a way to organize his thoughts, a reprieve from longer writing genres, and perhaps sometimes also an escape / a short holiday break. Undoubtedly, many (if not all) of these poems reflect greater ponds of dormant or developing stories, many of which may one day aspire to skip like rocks and converge—thus forming the foundation of a short story, novella or novel. Nonetheless, they are irrefutably expressions, thoughts, feelings and ideas that all together form Albert Russo—dancing, sobbing, ranting, raving, dreaming, reflecting, sometimes complicated and detailed, and at other times glistening with simple exuberance.

99

INTERVIEW QUESTIONS AND RESPONSES REGARDING
ALBERT RUSSO'S PROSE POETRY

I have several questions for Albert Russo regarding his prose poetry. They include: When did you first begin writing poetry? What / who were the influences in your life that resulted in your exploring poetry as an art form? Would you consider your poems to be a diary—of your ideas and thoughts, if not your "real life"? Did your parents encourage and/or discourage your desire to become a professional writer/author? Tell us about that. Many poets publish smaller poetry collections. You have published individual poems in several literary journals, but many of your most striking poems were saved for two big collections of your poetry: CWS2 and Gaytude. Please explain why. Which famous poets have inspired you, and why?

Here is Albert Russo's response:

"I may be repeating myself, but it is with poetry in English, that I started writing, and that goes back to my NYU years, in the beginning of the 1960's. Why poetry first? Because, not having any writing experience, except for a few dissertations I penned in French during my high-school years in Ruanda-Urundi (now two separate nations: Rwanda and Burundi, both having the same ethnic diversity, with, originally, the same percentages, i.e. about 79%, 19% and 2%, respectively: Hutu, Tutsi and Twa—pygmies), I felt like a sleeping volcano, and the words would erupt like simmering lava; in other words, nothing was premeditated. It was like an exorcism. All my pent-up anxiety, fears, rage, or whatever you may call it, burst out erratically. It all started thanks to a woman-friend painter and designer who introduced me to the artistic world of Greenwich Village. She gave me 'new wings with which to fly' into new and—to me—unheralded spaces. I had a strange feeling, both of vulnerability and exhilaration. If I was influenced—certainly—it must have been by the classical poets I had read and learned in my English, French, German and Dutch classes. So, no I have no specific poet in mind for that first period.

"Nowadays I still write poetry erratically, but with a thought or a subject in mind. For instance if I have seen something that disturbed me while watching the news, or if I have witnessed an incident in the street, or even a pleasant

occurrence, I have to jot down words about the things that have either pained or troubled me, as soon as I get back home. If, knowing that I have to wait a long time at the doctor's waiting-room, I carry a small note-book and a pen and write whatever passes through my mind at that moment. This seldom happens, for the presence of people around me is distracting. I could never create in a coffeeshop or a brasserie like some other writers do. Poetry remains an exorcism, I don't consider it a diary, even though it always revolves around my emotions and the reality that surrounds me. A diary has chronology, my poetry doesn't.

"My mother always supported me, actually her favorite literary genre was poetry, and she was one of my most loyal readers. I wouldn't say, best, since she could only be subjective. Her love of poetry was meshed with her love of her son. And this was a tremendous boon. My father, on the other hand, could not comprehend that writing was something to be taken seriously. And he did everything to discourage me from pursuing what he deemed to be a mere hobby. Yes, in spite of all his human qualities—he was a good, straight and generous man, loved by most people, no matter what color or creed; I owe him that side of his character, for in that way he was my mentor—I suffered my whole life because of his attitude, and this suffering continues, 35 years after his death, through nightmares, where he still reprimands me. Being an Agnostic, I may sound inconsistent, but I have the impression that he is somewhere and that he shows his disapproval by harassing me during my sleep.

"Before seeing my poems printed in the large CWS 2 volume—spanning 35-odd years of writing—and in 'Gaytude', and after having published in hundreds of literary and little magazines worldwide, I had maybe a dozen chapbooks that came out with small presses, mainly in the US, Canada and Great Britain, but also in France. Then, with age advancing and not knowing how long I would live, like everybody else who isn't suffering from a terminal disease, I felt the necessity of collecting my poetry and my prose in two big books. Going back to 'Gaytude', which I co-wrote with the excellent poet Adam Donaldson Powell, I should mention the fact that I had published previously, in French, 'Tour du Monde de la poésie gay' (TMPG), Editions Hors Commerce, Paris. Adam Donaldson Powell's contribution was new, whereas, I rewrote (not simply 'translated') in English all the poems included in TMPG. We then presented to the public a large bilingual book (in English and in French), accompanied by some of my own black and white erotic photos.

"The list of famous poets whom I love—does it mean that they have inspired me? Most probably yes—is so long that I can only cite them randomly, inasmuch as I read and continue to read them in their original English, French, Italian, Spanish and German native tongues. I still read, with more difficulty, Dutch-speaking poets. Whereas the other great poets who wrote in Russian, Chinese, Polish, Japanese, Korean, Tagalog, Hebrew, Arabic, Greek, Turkish, Persian, Creole, the numerous Indian and Nordic languages, etc. I have discovered in translation, in the five above-mentioned languages. Horace, Homer, Sophocles, Virgil, Ronsard, Shakespeare, R. Tagore, Apollinaire, Fray Luis de León, Chaucer, Dante, William Blake, Luis De Camoens, Malherbe, Robert Burns, Victor Hugo, Péguy, Lamartine, Baudelaire, Rimbaud, Verlaine, Aleksandr Blok, Maïakovski, Ossip Mandelstam, Fernando Pessoa, Nazim Hikmet, Paavo Haavikko, Emile Verhaeren, W.H. Auden, Walt Whitman, Allen Ginsberg, Pablo Neruda, Léopold Sédar Senghor, John Keats, Konstantin Kavafis, Stefan Anton George, Goethe, Rainer Maria Rilke, George Seferis, Borges, Pavese, Anna Akhmatova, William Wordsworth, Lord Byron, Shelley, Yeats, Emily Dickinson, E.E. Cummings, Robert Lowell, Edgar Allan Poe, Rudyard Kipling—I deem his poem 'If' to be one of the most meaningful and beautiful, anywhere, Edward Lear, T.S. Eliot, the German poets of the romantic 'Sturm und Drang' movement, Federico Garcia Lorca, Reinaldo Arenas, James Baldwin, John Cheever, Juan Goytisolo, Langston Hughes, Chinua Achebe, Umberto Saba, Charles Simic, Werner Lambersy whom I nominated for the prestigious Neustadt International Prize for Literature (which often leads to the Nobel Prize), reading 50-odd of his poetry books, etc… and I am still rereading classical or modern poets and discovering new ones. Inspiration is like delicious food that your taste buds remember, or a perfume you have long forgotten and whose whiff suddenly brushes your nostrils again, giving you pangs of nostalgia."

And I also posed some questions about "Gaytude" specifically: Please tell the readers "the inside story" of how "Gaytude" came to be—both in its previous form—and later. Has the publication of "Gaytude" underscored your reputation as being a "gay author" in the literary world? If so, has that been positive for you?

And here is Russo's response to those questions:

"As I mentioned previously, I first wrote 'Tour du monde de la poésie gay' in French. In that first version, I presented a world tour of gay people talking

about their lives, the difficulties of coming out, even in developed countries. Some of them spoke with rage, others affirmed their difference in a strong tone, still others concentrated on their sexual encounters, romantically, or with joy. As it was revealed, in the English / French edition published in the US with co-author Adam Donaldson Powell, all those people, with foreign names and varied experiences, which I 'translated', were in fact written by myself. I believe that in this book I used as many pen names as the great Portuguese writer Fernando Pessoa. It was an exhilarating exercise, close to what psychoanalysts call 'transference'.

"The reviews were excellent, and that made me happy, for I had really entered the soul of each of these men, women, transvestites and hermaphrodites. Was it a hoax? No, I wanted to measure myself with the LGBT minority in all kinds of situations. I hear some excellent authors say that we lie when we write. They can speak for themselves, I don't have the impression of lying, on the contrary, a part of me is revealed in each one of these 'transferences', whether it is in poetry or in fiction, inasmuch as I am incapable of writing a conventional, chronological autobiography. The moment I start doing that, I get 'seasick' and I want to throw up. So, what kind of a liar am I?

"I also wish to acknowledge an important fact—and it is not a mere detail: when I chose to publish the American edition of 'Gaytude' together with Adam Donaldson Powell, it wasn't just because he is a good friend, it is because his voice complements mine, and because I deem him to be a poet of superior quality. I have other friends who write and I would never invite them to share a book with me just because I like them. So much said for slanderers!

"Here too, I want to thank Delphine Lebensart of Editions Hors Commerce, in Paris, for having allowed me to tackle all the genres in which I write. She was the only publisher who saw my entire literary persona. Unfortunately, her outlet folded a decade ago, and I miss her and her vision of literature in all its aspects.

"I was proud to publish 'Gaytude' with Adam, and yes it was a very positive experience. I have nothing to hide, but again, if someone wishes to call me a gay author, then he or she is free to do so. I really don't mind, though I still prefer to be referred to merely as an author. I never liked labels, but in our society, people need references. I do understand that some gay men and women, and especially *adolescents, have to hold onto something that they can recognize, for a lot of them suffer from rejection within their family or their immediate environment.*

"I must admit though that it is only through the great number of laudatory gay reviews and articles that I understood how my books reverberated, and by the constant sales of my gay novels. No one approached me personally. Would young French gay people be more timid than their American or British counterparts? I often read their questions addressed to these journals, but they were mostly anonymous. Yes, they were scared to come out, and I understand them. Don't forget that LGBT suicides are four times as numerous as suicides of non-gay youths."

—⁂—

CROWDED WORLD OF SOLITUDE, VOLUME 1— COLLECTED SHORT STORIES AND ESSAYS

Among the many learned and creative writers who have collaborated with Albert Russo, written introductions to and/or have reviewed his work are Martin Tucker, Eric Tessier, David Alexander and Jean-Luc Breton.

Russo's Crowded World of Solitude, Volume 1 (his collected short stories) is prefaced with a wonderful essay by Martin Tucker, which also speaks in general terms about the literary genius of Albert Russo:

General introduction to Albert Russo's work by Martin Tucker.

"Albert Russo's art and life are all of a unique piece, and that piece is a plurality of cultures. Born in what was then the Belgian Congo and now is Congo/Zaire, he grew up in Central and Southern Africa and writes in both English and French, his two 'mother tongues'. With his intense interest in African life, the young Russo also engaged with knowledge beyond narrow stratifications of colonial custom. As a youth he left Africa for college in New York (where he attended New York University). For many years he has been resident in Paris.

"*Wherever he has lived, Russo has concerned himself with one hard-burning commitment: to achieve an illumination of vision in his writing that suggests by the force of its light some direction for understanding of human behavior and action. He draws on the many cultures he has been privileged to know, and he is always respectul of diversity. But Russo is no mere reporter. While he works with words, and while his work is concerned with place and the spirit of place, he is more interested in visitation than visits. Almost every fiction Russo has written involves a visitation, a hearing from another world that reverberates into a dénouement and revolution of the protagonist's present condition. These visitations are of course a form of fabulism—that is, utilizing the fable as a subtext of the animal nature of man. Russo's fabulism, however, is not in the line of traditional mythology (perhaps mythologies is a better term, since Russo draws from a variety of folklore and consummate literary executions). In one of his recent fictions, for example, he writes of a man who falls in love with a tree-- his love is so ardent he wills himself into a tree in order to root out any foreignness in his love affair. Thus, Russo's "family tree", the mating of woodland Adam and Eve, becomes in his creation not only a multicultural act but a cross-fertilization of the cultures he has drawn from. In this personal fable Russo suggests the Greek myth of Pan love and even the Adamastor legend, that Titan who has turned cruelly into a rock out of unbridled passion for a goddess. Russo suggests other legends as well, and certainly the crossing of boundaries, psychological, emotional as well as physical and territorial--hybrid phenomena now sweeping into the attention of all of Africa and the Middle East--is to be found within the feelingful contours of his tale.*

"*Fabulism is now a recognized presence in our literary lives. It goes by other names: magic realism is one of them. Underneath all the manifestations of this phenomenon is the artistic credo that creation is larger than life, and that the progeny created enhances the life that gave being to it. In sum, the artist is saying that life is larger than life if given the opportunity to be lived magnificently. Russo's is certainly a part of this willingness to experiment beyond the observable. His fiction represents, in essence, a belief, in the endless perceivable possibilities of mind. Its humor is at times dark, however, and perhaps this color of mood is a reflection of Russo's background and biography. For his art, while enlarging, is not showered with sun. His dark hues are those of ironic vision.*

"Russo may be said to be very much a part of the beginning of this century. His concentration is on the inevitabilities of unknowingness; thus his resort is to the super-rational as a way of steadying himself in the darkness. At the same time his work cannot be said to be tragic, for the unending endings of his fictions suggest a chance of progress, if not completion of one's appointed task, worlds meet and become larger worlds in Russo's work; people change within his hands.

"It is a pleasure to pay homage to Russo's achievement."

The enormity and scale of genres comprising Albert Russo's total literary production is astounding, and perhaps difficult to sum up in a few sentences. However, Mr. Tucker has really hit the nail on its head with these sentences in particular, which are well worth repeating: "He draws on the many cultures he has been privileged to know, and he is always respectful of diversity. But Russo is no mere reporter. While he works with words, and while his work is concerned with place and the spirit of place, he is more interested in visitation than visits. Almost every fiction Russo has written involves a visitation, a hearing from another world that reverberates into a dénouement and revolution of the protagonist's present condition. These visitations are of course a form of fabulism—that is, utilizing the fable as a subtext of the animal nature of man. Russo's fabulism, however, is not in the line of traditional mythology (perhaps mythologies is a better term, since Russo draws from a variety of folklore and consummate literary executions)."

Jean-Luc Breton, in his review "About The Age of the Pearl" (World Literature Today, 2002), has aptly written: "Science fiction and fantasy are the paths trodden by Albert Russo in his quest for a pre-Babel reconciliation of man with himself in all his constitutive dimensions, linguistic and social, but also generic and transcendental. Generic distinction is, for Russo as for Aristophanes in Plato's Symposium, akin to the loss of perfection. " And in his review "About Beyond the Water" (World Literature Today, 2001), he has also written: "All of Mr Russo's readers know that he can write as easily about his native Africa as about present-day New York or Italy in the sixties; and the collection, with stories set in different places and milieus, highlights his especial talent at transporting his readers from one scene to another, in a kind of "sentimental journey" through human experience. Mostly, this is performed through the use of one—or sometimes several—narrator(s) whose identity and standpoint are not revealed to us in the opening lines of the story where he / she / they appear(s). Mr Russo's favourite device is projecting his readers in medias res, usually at a crucial moment."

Of course, this collection of short stories and essays begins with several short stories that take place in Africa. Jean-Luc Breton's comment that all of Russo's readers know that he can write easily about his native Africa is echoed in comments written by Eric Tessier and and Edmund White regarding his African-novel trilogy "The Benevolent American in the Heart of Darkness":

"In Albert Russo's Africa you will find humankind's infinite diversity and, amid such richness, a quest for the deep self."—Eric Tessier.

"Albert Russo has recreated through a young African boy's joys and struggles many of the tensions of modern life, straight and gay, black and white, third world and first ... all of these tensions underlie this story of a biracial child adopted by a benevolent American. Mixed Blood or Your son Leopold is a non-stop, gripping read!"—Edmund White.

This book won an Honorable Mention in the 13th Annual Writer's Digest International Self-Published Book Awards, Mainstream Fiction Category. Here are the judge's comments: "The Crowded World, indeed. One gets the sense that Russo has been everywhere, done everything, seen everything, and then turned around and written about it in these stories. What I like most about this collection (and it's only Volume One!) is its variety—there are stories set in Africa, stories for children, essays, science fiction, fantasy... In short, this is one writer who is incredibly diverse, and seems to be able to do a remarkable number of different things. There are some extravagant sex scenes, which are quite difficult to do without becoming quickly absurd. All in all, a really terrific collection, with some lovely prose."

The book contains six parts: African stories, Mainstream stories, Juvenile literature, Essays, Fantasy and Science-fiction, and The Ripov Series. These six parts include the following works:

PART ONE—AFRICAN STORIES: THE EXAMINATION, TUNISIAN FEVER, THE WET HIDING, BEYOND THE GREAT WATER, THE DISCOVERY, A

STRANGER AT HOME, SOUK SECRETS, MAGIC FINGERS, SPIRIT OF TAR, and THE THIRD LINK.

PART TWO—MAINSTREAM STORIES: THE SEPHARDIC SISTERS, PARENTHESIS, THE CHOICE, ENTENTE CORDIALE, BRIDGES OF SIGHS, MARINA VELCOVA AND THE TEMPTATION OF AMERICA, TWENTY-ONE DAYS IN THE LIFE OF A CURISTE AT CONSTIPAX-LES-BAINS, FRANCE, GLASNOST AND THE GOLEM, THE DILEMMA, RUE DE SEINE, A HELL OF AN EVENING, MEMORY GAP, TO OUR LADY OF THE FIELDS—LORRAINE, FRANCE, MILANESE INTERMEZZO, LEBENSBORN, FLAVIO'S DILEMMA, MUHDAH AT CASTLE WELL, VENITIAN THRESHOLDS, SMALL TALK, UNMASKING HEARTS, THE SPELL OF MAYALAND, FAST FOOD LISETTE, MEXICAN FAREWELL, NEW YORK BONUS, DOGGEDLY YOURS, and MURMURS IN THE SISTINE CHAPEL.

PART THREE—JUVENILE LITERATURE: HEIST, THE WAY IT IS, PIANO LESSONS, THE CHRISTMAS REPORT, and THE BREAK.

PART FOUR—ESSAYS: IONESCO IN ACTION / TRIAL BY JURY: FROM THE INSIDE, IN THE CRADLE OF SERENDIB, MURDER OF A NOVEL PARISIAN STYLE, AMID THE FRENZY OF FRANCE'S MERRY-GO-ROUND, and PASSAGES.

PART FIVE—FANTASY AND SCIENCE-FICTION: THE CRIMSON ISLAND, THE MUSICHOR, HARRY'S PERPETUATORS, THE EMO CONVERT, STILL-LIFE REVOLT, CHINCHERINCHEES, VARIATION ON SADKO, QUIRK, REPENT, THE TARGET, THE VINDICTIVE STUDIO, IN TRANSIT, ARTICLE ONE ELEVEN, THE RAZOR'S EDGE, RETURN TO THE SOURCE, THE AGE OF THE PEARL, IN THE NICK OF TIME, SPYING INCIDENT, GRANPA RODNEY'S MISSION, and BEYOND THE WILL.

PART SIX—THE RIPOV SERIES: MR. FATHER & RIPOV, APPLES & RIPOV, DOG TALK & RIPOV, THE BUS RIDE & RIPOV, FRANÇOIS DE RIPOVE, ROOTS & RIPOV, WIGS & RIPOV, LETTERS & RIPOV, THE AYATOLLAH & RIPOV, BUGGYLOVE & RIPOV, EFFICIENCY & RIPOV, GOODNESS GRACIOUS, RIPOV, SILIKITS & RIPOV, CHIPS & RIPOV, SEMANTICS & RIPOV, SYMBOLS & RIPOV, BILLY-DOC & RIPOV, and KRITIX & RIPOV.

I will reproduce three short works for the readers, add a few of my own comments, and then pose questions to Albert Russo. The stories that I have selected are: "Beyond the Great Water" (African stories), "The Age of the Pearl" (Fantasy and Science-fiction stories), and "Apples and Ripov" (The Ripov Series).

BEYOND THE GREAT WATER

first appeared in Short Story International (USA)

Regarding "Beyond the Great Water" Jean-Luc Breton has written the following synopsis of this story in his review "About Beyond the Great Water" (World Literature Today, 2001):

"Unexpectedness is one of the main motifs of Albert Russo's short stories. Beyond the Great Water, for example, is built on the gradual development of the American dream of an African child, followed by the sudden anticlimax of a plane crash. Only one letter survives the accident, and its contents reveal to the little boy the tragic coincidence of the fulfilment of his hope of meeting his American benefactor and the death of the latter."

Having done his homework and fulfilled the household chores, Ilongo forked the crossbar of his Belgian-made bicycle and pedalled his way along the footpath that snaked through the tall grass. The rain had stopped and he breathed in the thick, pea-scented air, letting it slowly, sensuously, seep into his lungs as if it were an elixir.

No sooner had the tires of the Flandria hugged the asphalt than Ilongo gathered speed. He cleaved the atmosphere and spread his arms wing-like, shifting the weight of his hips in a regular sway so as to keep his balance, ready for an imaginary takeoff. He could now clearly view the lake with the fawn-tinted mountain range kneeling on the opposite bank like a multi-humped lioness. Ilongo often dreamt of hovering above the dozing beast so that he could vie with Mungu in the daily task of ministering to his earthly creatures, a task which did not preclude occasional outbursts of wrath, such as the lightning that struck a neighboring village the other day, for how else would people be reminded of Mungu's presence?

Cycling towards the airdrome was the lad's favorite pastime. He would watch the kitenge-clad women pick cotton while, close to a shed, boys barely older than he pressed the fluffy white bolls into wicker baskets. On the other side of the road stretched a paddy-field where other women toiled, bent over, their ankles deep in the water. Ilongo felt exhilarated at the sight of such industriousness.

Not long ago the schoolmaster had lectured on the land, its produce, stressing the importance of coffee in the nation's economy. He'd explained that both arabica and robusta beans were of such high grade that the bulk was exported to the United States of America, bringing in return much needed foreign currency. This, to Ilongo, had been somewhat of a revelation, for America was the country where Baba Paul Leroy Smith lived. Baba Paul was Ilongo's foster father, thanks to whom the lad was encouraged to pursue his schooling and to learn—later on—a useful profession. When, in one of his letters, Baba Paul had asked whether he already had an idea of what he wanted to do in the future, llongo mentioned the civil service and spoke of Uncle Tambe. Uncle Tambe, a senior clerk at the post office in the capital, was a much respected man, even with the elders, and he could also type with two fingers.

But it was between broadcasting and aviation that Ilongo's heart swayed. Whenever he had the opportunity, Ilongo would borrow the Philips transistor from Diluwe. He enjoyed listening to the frenzied beat of the local music and to the latest French or American songs, but nothing interested him more than the news. The voices of the man and of the woman would alternate to inform him of the events, small or shattering, through which Mungu manifested his moods. He liked to believe that he was being addressed personally and drank the words with a mixture or relish and fascination. He pictured himself before a microphone speaking, as the Messenger, to all and sundry in a tone of voice at once vibrant and confidential. No matter how sad the news might be, he would win the admiration of thousands of listeners.

Ilongo the pilot was the other image that flashed in the schoolboy's mind especially when, as now, he was riding parallel to the runway. The pot-bellied air force Bréguet squatted at its habitual place nonchalantly behind a DC 3. Except for the few cars stationed in the parking lot, there was no sign of the imminent arrival or the plane coming from Europe. Ilongo always waited with the same pinch of emotion for the moment the gleaming object would pierce through the horizon, gradually taking form, in total silence at first, then with a rumble that would stretch into a long-drawn whine. How majestic the white and blue aircraft would appear as it would initiate its descent, making no more noise than would be necessary, as if mindful not to disturb the peace of Mungu.

110

"The plane must have been delayed again," the young boy concluded, disappointed, as he watched the evening set in after the dusk's swift and blazing interlude.

He hadn't noticed the hour go by. The crickets had begun their stupid din, trying as forcefully as they could to drown the concert of rumors which had accompanied the brightening of the moon. Yonder the lake shimmered as if star powder was being sprinkled on the surface. Each one of these flickering lights was a fishing boat. Early in the morning at the soko the fish stalls would display their rows of fleshy banga-bangas still agape, as if even dead they wanted to lure you, and the glistening dakalas, those tiny fishes the size of a child's finger which deep-fried one chews whole: head, tail, and bone.

Ilongo suddenly perked his ears then realized the gurgle came from his own stomach. He'd just remembered that for dinner he'd had the leftovers of yesterday's chicken mwambe. Shangazi—Auntie—always cooked generous portions of mwambe which she served with manioc dough and hibiscus leaves when there were guests like the ndukus—relatives—from the hills who were staying with them for a couple of days. Ilongo wondered whether Baba Paul ate the same kind of food or preferred beefsteak with salad and French fries of which the Europeans here seemed so fond.

Baba Paul's last letter dated from a month and a half ago. In it he'd said that Ilongo should prepare himself for a lovely surprise. Last year's money order had permitted Ilongo to buy the second-hand bicycle. Although he hadn't gone through the rites of manhood yet, with the Flandria, Ilongo felt he'd entered the adult world.

As the eldest child of the household, Ilongo helped Shangazi take care of her three children. His mama had died giving birth to him. Soon after her death, Ilongo's father married Shangazi but Ilongo could hardly remember him as Shangazi had chased him away a long time ago. Shangazi still referred to her husband as the good-for-nothing who'd spent his time running after loose women and wasted the family's meager resources drinking pombe. Actually Ilongo didn't miss not having his real father around.

Baba Paul had more than replaced him, for not only was Baba Paul Ilongo's father—it said so in the document the young boy kept with his school reports— but he also provided for Shangazi and her children. Shangazi pretended that the good spirits had taken pity on her, shutting up old Mapindi once and for all.

Mapindi, who was Diluwe's grandmother, had once cast a spell on her. "Doomed you are," she'd said, "for you shall remain without a husband and because of you the foreigner from Beyond the Great Water shall be consumed by fire."

Jealousy had poisoned Mapindi's tongue since now the old woman had become completely mute. She continued to curse with her eyes though and whenever Shangazi had to go and fetch water from the river (Mapindi's hut stood at the edge of the pathway), she'd spit on the ground wishing that those vicious orbs would be plunged into eternal darkness.

Time and again Shangazi had warned her nephew not to go near the hut of Mapindi's family, but they were the only ones in the village who owned a transistor radio; Ilongo found it very difficult to obey. In fact, Ilongo who had never questioned his love for Shangazi believed that she was an easy prey to superstition and that her fears of the old woman were a bit ridiculous.

That night, after making certain the children and Shangazi were asleep, Ilongo brought the oil-lamp to the head of his mat and opened the round tin box containing Baba Paul's letters. The lad chose one at random and as he began reading it he felt a pinch at the base of his heart. He went on to the next letter and then to the next, and by the time he'd put back the lid over the tin box and turned off the flame inside the oil-lamp, he'd gone through the whole correspondence and contemplated the hand-colored portrait of his foster father.

Lulled by the soft purring of the sleepers, Ilongo drifted into that borderless expanse which lies between wakefulness and dream and which, high in the fabled Mountains of the Moon, is Mungu's retreat. On the surface of the lake of clouds loomed the face of Baba Paul, huge and seemingly awash. As his lips began to move, the mountain peaks started to shake, looking like fangs slicing the air. A voice could now be heard deep and cavernous and so very weary it must have traveled all the way from the centre of the earth. The voice spoke a language unintelligible to Ilongo, yet there was something familiar and awesome about it. Mungu had strange ways of addressing humans; that was why there were witch doctors to interpret his messages.

At the far end of the lake of clouds, another face appeared but much smaller than Baba Paul's, it was toothless old Mapindi, dusty and wrinkled like the ground in the dry season, and yet she was beaming. Then a crow flew in and *pecked at Mapindi's eyes all the while the old woman continued to laugh. Soon though the whole cloud and mountain-scape vanished under the crow's wings.*

Riding to school the next morning, Ilongo thought intently about Baba Paul. It was composition day and he had the feeling that he was going to write about his foster father. That strong, sudden urge took Ilongo by surprise, for although it was no mystery that he and his family had a provider, until now the lad had been very guarded when people questioned him about Baba Paul. And in any case, Ilongo had never been the boastful type. Could the dream have prompted such a change in attitude? "I'm getting superstitious like Shangazi, aya!" he grinned. Not quite convinced, he spat towards the ground but instead, the blob landed on the rim of the wheel.

At school, the teacher made the announcement before the class that during the night a great tragedy had occurred. The plane coming from Europe which had been expected late in the afternoon had crashed in the jungle of Sudan. The investigators would have to locate the site of the accident but it was feared that there wouldn't be any survivors. For days, all over the land, the conversation revolved around the plane crash. In the middle of the week, the two local newspapers released pictures of the scattered remains of the aircraft. The black box, however, hadn't been recovered. In the village the speculations abounded. One elder claimed it was a revenge of the martyrs' souls against the colonialists. To this argument a younger man retorted, "And how about our own nationals who happened to be aboard, returning students most of them?" The elder clicked his tongue, "They had no business leaving the soil of their forebears to come back and sow venomous ideas among our population. As it is, there are enough ministers parading with their ndukus and wives in expensive new cars and filling their homes with devilish instruments. Have our youth lost all sense or pride? Whoever finds that black box had better be warned, for the spirits inhabiting it will strike him and they won't spare his kin either. Spirits do not tolerate disrespect."

Ilongo kept thinking of Baba Paul, every one of his nights now became crowded with images of his benefactor. They were mainly peaceful images but nonetheless, it started to weigh inside the lad's chest. And also, he did not like the way Mapindi croaked each time people spoke of the plane accident. He'd noticed how awkwardly she'd glance at him as if she were rejoicing about some evil deed. "Nonsense," he exclaimed to himself, dismissing the idea that she'd cast him a spell, "the old woman is just losing her mind."

On Friday, the schoolmaster gave back the corrected compositions and Ilongo was praised for having written the best paper. He was invited to read it aloud in front of the class. Ilongo felt at once flattered and uneasy. Was it right to display in public that privileged relationship? Anyway, it was too late now, and with contained emotion, Ilongo read his composition. Thus it was that his fellow students learned about Paul Leroy Smith, an Afro-American who resided in New Orleans, in the southern state of Louisiana, that this man who worked as a pharmacist in a drugstore, was a bachelor, and that he devoted what spare time he had to civil rights activities, because he could not forget that his grandparents had once been slaves. Paul Leroy Smith had marched with a great black leader named Martin Luther King who had died for the cause of his people, just like Lumumba and other great Africans who had fought the wars of independence. Wishing to resuscitate the link with his African heritage, Paul Leroy Smith had become Ilongo's foster father.

Late one afternoon. as he was tying the chain of his Flandria to the pole outside the family hut, Ilongo saw Diluwe run in his direction.

"A letter from America," Diluwe said, panting, 'it's for you. It was found among the debris of the plane."

Staring at the envelope, llongo was aghast. The upper left corner was charred and on the lighter patch below one could clearly distinguish a fingerprint as if someone had wanted to stop the fire from spreading. A chill coursed Ilongo's spine as he opened the letter. Diluwe stood by, eager to hear what the news was all about. Ilongo silently read the portion of the letter that had escaped the flames. In the last paragraph Baba Paul announced that he was about to fulfill his dearest wish, he was coming to Africa to meet him. And here was his travel schedule; he'd fly from New Orleans to New York, there he'd catch the transatlantic flight to Brussels, he'd stay overnight in the Belgian capital, then board the plane for U.

Fate had decided that the letter accompany its sender. Thus had the soul of Baba Paul returned to the continent of his ancestors.

THE AGE OF THE PEARL

appeared in Orbis Magazine (UK) winner of the Readers' fiction award and in Short Story International (USA)

Jean-Luc Breton has written the following comments regarding "The Age of the Pearl" in his review "About The Age of the Pearl" (World Literature Today, 2002): "The pervading feeling, when one reads through The Age of the Pearl, is that of human unworthiness; and the relevance of the fictional alienation brought by fantasy and science-fiction is obvious. This alienation is best exposed in the title story, in which Albert Russo's dialectical exploration of sense and the senses centres on the metaphor of the pearls, coveted objects of artificial beauty, colourful, changing, contradictory, profuse, created in amazing numbers, ironically spewed out onto our shores by millions of oysters and slowly choking humankind away from Earth. The humans in the story can only choose between death by profusion and death by sterility, just because of their initial greed and vanity."

David Alexander has commented (in his book review entitled "The stories of Albert Russo: Crystals in a Shock Wave") that the story "The Age of the Pearl" "... again deals with a case of sweeping metamorphosis in the form of grotesque and bizarre consequences when the innocuous assumes the dimensions of monstrous evil. Slowly and inexorably, by an alien, inhuman and implacable process, the seas' oysters are wildly, cancerously multiplying to the point where they must soon overwhelm the natural barriers of earth and ocean. By the attrition of sheer force of numbers, humanity is doomed. The very world, it seems, has developed cancer, and there is no cure in sight."

Strolling along the nacreous stretch of a South Pacific islet were an ageing man and a female child. They were both naked and holding hands. "Tell me again, great-grandpa," the little girl inquired, "why is it that we cannot go into the sea? When I look at the water and know I cannot dip my feet in it I feel terribly sad," The centenarian gazed silently at the turquoise expanse. Beads of perspiration rimmed his lash-less eyes. Was there a tear among them? "Great-grandpa," the little girl said impatiently, "you haven't answered me. All you do when you come here is stare at the ocean. I won't come any more."

The old man gently patted the child's shoulder. Still fixing the aqueous immensity, he began to talk as if to himself.

"It goes back so many years. As a matter of fact, the last time I remember having swum I must have been your age. And this beach had real sand. You could feel its fluffiness under your toes. But the sea, Krela, the sea," the old man lamented, "it was so incredibly beautiful and soothing. I'd dive in it and swim for hours on end. Deep under the water, along the coral reef, I'd open my eyes and suddenly there was magic: the glass sponge so hospitable yet so discreet, the pink-eyed indicus with its razor-teeth, pious like a bald monk, the atolla lighting up as if it were a Christmas tree, the octopus-weed graceful as a ballerina, stroking shades of a diabolic dance. The sea-fan, the wonder-lamp and, oh, Krela, the silver-fins, they would lead me to the secret entrances of the Low Realm. A living treasure trove, Krela!"

"But great-grandpa," Krela whispered, reverent and incredulous at once, "are you all right?" The centenarian lowered his eyes and smoothed Krela's blond curls with the palm of his hand. "You think I've lost my mind, don't you? No, I'm not raving, I have seen them just as I see you now."

Krela gaped in wonderment. He spoke so passionately about everything that she only half believed whatever he said. He'd come up with such amazing tales. Though he did appear quite lucid and had a vast knowledge of the universe, Krela was certain that her great-grandpa embellished his memories in a most fantastic manner. But she loved it, for he provided her with worlds she couldn't reach, even in her dreams. Once in a while he'd mention the scourge of the pearls. And he'd become extremely despondent. Nevertheless, he'd promised to tell her all about it. And this is how he finally recounted the story, using at times words and definitions that sounded totally outlandish to her.

"Long, long ago, pearls were a rarity indeed. To find a handful of them you had to gather thousands of oysters. It would take weeks, even months, and people would die in search of a pearl. Generally they'd drown. Do you know what a pearl is made of Krela? It is an iridescent concretion produced by certain marine and freshwater molluscs. It is composed almost entirely of nacre, or

116

mother of-pearl, the compound which forms the inner layer of mollusc shells. A pearl, the only gem of animal origin, results from an abnormal growth of nacre around minute particles of foreign matter such as sand.

Let me also tell you about the oysters. These have separate sexes. Eggs and sperm are shed into the water, and after fertilization, the embryo develops into a free-swimming larva with rudiments of a shell and a bundle of cilia for propulsion and feeding. As the shell enlarges, the veliger develops. This second larval form has a well-muscled foot, a bivalve shell and internal organs. The spat, i.e. the young oyster, remains free-swimming for some two weeks before settling down and attaching itself to a suitable surface. Some bivalves go through a brief parasitic phase that aids dispersal. The larva of these species must attach itself to a fish for development to take place. Afterward, the young bivalve abandons its host to take up an independent existence in the ocean. As I told you before, natural pearls were extremely rare, until a Japanese—his name was Kokichi Mikimoto—devised a method of cultivating pearls artificially. Mikimoto had to tackle a number of biology and marine-science related problems first. The red tide was one of them. The increase in plankton which tainted the sea blood red would kill the oysters by the millions. Then there were the octopi and the cold underwater currents. But our indefatigable Japanese fought relentlessly against the odds. Invention succeeded invention. He obtained hemispherical pearls initially, then one day, from the shell of a dead oyster, he extracted a perfectly round gem. He cut the pearl in half and discovered in its center the spherical nucleus which he had originally implanted. Kokichi Mikimoto pursued his research, improving both the color and the lustre of his pearls. But it was by accelerating the growth function of oysters that Mikimoto revolutionized aquatic life.

Never had he suspected the magnitude of his discovery and least of all its outcome. For it reached far beyond the mere multiplication of cultured pearls. Those pearls which adorned the delicate necks of women around the globe. To counter the murderous red tides, Mikimoto used culturing baskets and platforms, attaching baby shells as a means of propagating oysters. And now, Krela, the pearls to which an industrious Japanese had devoted his life are as common as the grains of sand in the desert. They have washed ashore to cover all the beaches that lace our continents and the myriad isles such as the one we are both standing on. There was sand here once, and pebbles too, but these have disappeared under layers of pearls. The white, black, pale blue and indigo pearls we're so accustomed to."

"Great-grandpa, it's all very fascinating, about the pearls and the oysters, I mean," Krela said in a tone of expectation, "But you haven't explained why I can't swim in the ocean the way you used to. Is it dangerous?" The old man, obviously strained, walked the child to a flat rock on a promontory, made himself comfortable and produced two ripe mangoes from a bag. He motioned the child to sit next to him and handed her a fruit. They both relished their snack, biting voluptuously into its juicy flesh. Krela had already finished hers while the centenarian was still savoring the oblong fruit, licking its seed dry. Now that he had gathered new energy, he went on to satisfy the child's curiosity.

"I would come to this very place, dive into the sea and look for oysters. I'd bring back home basketfuls of them and we'd eat them raw. They were tender and delicious," the old man smiled, pinching Krela's cheek, "just like you! But this has changed. Do you know that humans traveled on the oceans and even lived under the water in what used to be called bathyspheres? For centuries we were masters of the seas. But in fact we knew so little about them. Today it is the ocean that rules us. The only thing we're allowed is to contemplate it and pump limited quantities of water, filtering and desalinating it for our daily needs."

"Have we done anything wrong, great-grandpa, that made the ocean so angry against us?" the child asked, looking quite puzzled.

"Yes, Krela, we have abused it, we have dumped tons of refuse in it, poisoning part of its life, killing some of its most valuable creatures and flora. And it took revenge, confining us to our land. We have become the seas' prisoners, Krela. Before, we needed each other like parent and child, brother and sister, man and woman. Before, there were rivers that flowed inland, rivers in which we could bathe and fish, some of them thousands of kilometres long. They are all dried up now. As a result, mankind depends on the good will of the seas. We have turned into orphans, Krela. And soon we shall have to look for another planet to settle on, lest we are reduced to parasites." Krela listened dumbfounded to the centenarian's predicament. Her eyes pleaded, "Surely we will find a way to save everybody?"

Then, in the old man's mouth, the words 'pearl' and 'oyster' exploded successively. "You're so young, Krela, but you ought to know nevertheless.

Thanks to Mikimoto the oysters have proliferated, unchecked, covering every reef and incline under the oceans, damming all the estuaries. Oysters have grown to be the most populous species of our universe. What's more, they have learned to mass-produce pearls naturally, expelling them from their organisms, strewing them over our shores so as to create a permanent barrier between land and sea. Their ultimate aim, Krela, is to eliminate the earth's population, animal and plant alike. Every year they ration the water flow at the rate of ten percent. And we humans have no alternative but to explore the galaxy for our survival. By the time you reach adulthood, you won't be living here any longer."

"But what are the oysters doing in the ocean?" inquired Krela, unperturbed by an event which seemed to her far removed in the future.

"They're building huge mazes underwater to safeguard the sea inhabitants. Imagine walls of oysters, scaffoldings, bridges of oysters. That's what they're doing. And sooner than we'd want it to happen, they'll be sealing off all that blue horizon you are gazing at. You can't notice it, Krela, for they're just below the surface. It's only a matter of years before they accomplish their project."

Krela's face suddenly glowed: "Then we'll be able to walk on the water, great-grandpa! It'll be the most beautiful day of my life."

The old man nodded, forcing a smile. "Why not," he acknowledged to himself, "why not."

~

APPLES & RIPOV

Ripov lived in a shoddy tenement house which faced the I.O.U. Insurance building, a sparkling curvilinear structure whose bronze-hued mirrors greedily absorbed the daylight. Every morning after he'd opened the curtains, Ripov would stare at the building with ecstatic eyes. Not exactly a pariah, Ripov limited his diet to four meals a week. By his demeanor and by the way he dressed, no one would suspect his actual social status. And he would not have had it otherwise. He would do a few odd jobs occasionally, and then just to cover his modest needs. The rent of his mouse hole did not amount to much, and, though he did not eat like most people, Ripov knew his body's requirements almost to the calorie.

Tall, well-groomed, and quite handsome, Ripov fit the description of the aggressive young executive that a success-oriented society so avidly feeds on. Ripov held no bank account, no insurance policy, nor for that matter did he abide by the rigid laws of consumerism. And yet he always managed to remain within the confines of legality. A feat he could only be proud of inasmuch as he was spared the qualms of the Internal Revenue: they couldn't claim anything from him: he was penniless. On the other hand, Ripov was endowed with an iron constitution. But how happy or unhappy was he? That he kept a tightly sealed secret. But one thing Ripov couldn't resist was apples, and I.O.U.'s trademark was a Golden Delicious surmounted by a Granny Smith.

One afternoon Ripov decided he would go and inquire about the sign. There were half-a-dozen people waiting in the lobby ... and a basketful of apples at each side of the entrance. Two businessmen and a young lady were leafing through magazines while nonchalantly munching on an apple. Ripov swallowed several times before he approached the basket containing the Golden Delicious. As he was about to select one, a doubt arose in his mind and instantly glued his lips together. He eyed the Granny Smiths at the left of the entrance. The receptionist, meanwhile, juggled the intercom and two telephone receivers, passing on messages and announcing visitors. There was a constant flow of people in and out of the lobby so that Ripov's presence there remained unnoticed (or, I should say, perfectly warranted). Finally, he grabbed a Golden Delicious, rolled it against his trousers and let it slip into the pocket of his jacket, covering the bulge by drumming his fingers over it in an impatient, business-like fashion. Between a call and an announcement, the receptionist addressed Ripov. "Whom did you wish to see, Sir?" Instead of answering, the would-be client stretched out his arm and pensively glanced at his watch, signifying that he was late, thereafter gesturing that he'd come back some other time. As he swung the door behind him, Ripov heard the receptionist's last words: "Your name, Sir?"

Two days later at about the same hour, Ripov was sitting in the I.O.U. lobby, this time next to the basket of Granny Smiths. After a moment's hesitation, he selected an apple, felt its firmness, then munched at it as naturally as he could, feigning not to mind the bustle around him. When his turn came to be announced (by then he'd eaten half of his Granny Smith) Ripov stood up, gallantly let a lady client go to the desk before him and, nodding his head towards the lobby's futuristic clock, left the premises.

This went on for a couple of weeks. And though by now the receptionist recognized Ripov, smiling at him upon his arrival, she was obviously too busy to run after the now familiar stranger as the latter inevitably pointed at his watch. Or thus thought Ripov. Until it happened that, suddenly, and though by magic, the lobby emptied itself, leaving him alone with the receptionist. The sweet taste of the Golden Delicious soured in his palate.

With a sigh of relief the girl said, "At long last! How many months has it been now? I was afraid you'd lose patience. You wouldn't imagine the nights I spent thinking you'd give up on me. The subtle pretext of having to leave when it came to your turn. Oh, darling, we don't even know each other's name." Tears of laughter filled the girl's eyes as she added: "And the way you kept munching at those silly apples!"

'Silly apples ... silly apples...' The phrase bounced up and down Ripov's throat like a puppet's hiccough as he scampered away through the streets of his neighborhood.

—ฺ๑ฺ๑—

AUTHOR'S COMMENTS ABOUT THE STORIES, AND MORE QUESTIONS FOR ALBERT RUSSO

In this massive volume Russo shows his aptitude as an entertainer—pleasing the reader with all kinds of drama, humor, and sometimes even a hint of sardonic wit. In many of Russo's works I sense commentaries about the status quo, and the difficulties involved in resisting it in all its expressions. Although Russo writes about many issues and experiences that are sobering, he also has quite a light and humorous side and writes in such a way that the reader ends up not only chuckling at the characters in the stories but also at himself/herself. My favorites among these stories (as noted by the excerpts chosen) are "Beyond the Great Water", "The Age of the Pearl" and "Apples and Ripov". However, there are many other jewels in Russo's treasure trove which also should be read—and some warrant second readings.

My final questions for Albert Russo about his short story and essay collection Crowded World of Solitude, Volume One are:

1) Can you tell us about how you got the idea for the character Ripov, and if he is based upon a real-life person, or a composite of real-life persons? I personally associate the name "Ripov" with the Czech Republic, and I thus wonder if you see any similarities in the mindsets and styles between these works and those of Milan Kundera and/or Franz Kafka? Here I am thinking of your usage of humor, the depiction of the absurdities of the status quo, and the inevitability of its endurance.

2) Several specific persons have often been associated with your works—both as co-authors, collaborators, reviewers and more. These include Martin Tucker, David Alexander, Eric Tessier and Jean-Luc Breton. Please tell the readers about your relationships/collaborations with these persons: how have you become acquainted with one another, how have you collaborated, and how have these persons enriched your life and writing?

3) The essays in this collection are very much like short stories. In much of your writing—not only your essays—I see elements of the expository, the descriptive, the narrative, and the persuasive. What is your own definition of an essay, and how does the writing experience differ from that of a short-short story?

4) Are there not some stories and characters that you have written about and created that are essentially hauntingly "alive" for you, and whose voices are perhaps now an integrated part of who you are? Here I am not just thinking of Zapinette, Ripov and the many personalities readers have come to know and love in your African novels, but also the psychology, and the fight for identity and raison d'être, of many of the characters in some of your "lesser" works. Will these literary archetypes survive you? What do you imagine will be your "literary heritage"—your African novels and short stories, your Zapinette series, your Ripov series, your poetry … ?

Here are Albert Russo's answers to my questions:

"Concerning Ripov, that absurd hero who always has good intentions but then always gets 'ripped off' by the people he meets or by his environment, I

would rather cite the Belgian-born and idiosyncratic surrealist Henri Michaux, whose hero 'Plume' I had studied and even played in the theater in Paris—my French theater director at the time during which I was an 'actor', had us read all the adventures of 'Plume', and she herself had adapted several episodes for the theater. Actually, now that I think of it, Ripov became, maybe unconsciously, the precursor of Zapinette.

"I knew Martin Tucker, from my second New York stay—he was then President of the American Pen Center in Manhattan. We became, and are still, very good friends. He is a highly respected poet, a professor of Literature in the widest sense, since he wrote books about British, American, African-American and African literature. He had read all of my African novels and wrote essays on them. He also penned several biographies, including that of Joseph Conrad and of Sam Shepard, the writer and actor. He was the Editor Emeritus of the excellent review Confrontation, the first journal which published episodes of Zapinette, among other works of mine.

"David Alexander, who lives in Brooklyn, NY, is also a good friend of mine. We met through his former wife, Judith Ammann, during one of their visits in Paris. She is a staunch feminist, who included some of my Ripov stories in a bilingual, German-English anthology, entitled 'Who's been sleeping in my brain', for which she was the main editor. It was published by the famous Suhrkamp Verlag. David is also an excellent poet and a famous author of thrillers—he is especially knowledgeable about the US secret services and American weaponry, air, land and water. He edited a whole issue of the Literary Review dedicated to the city of Venice, Italy. Here too, he included one of my Venetian stories. He then began to write long and sophisticated reviews on my books.

"Eric Tessier published me regularly in his magazine 'La nef des fous'. He also wrote many reviews of my books, and I encouraged him to publish stories in English (which I corrected), and now he appears in the same American and Indian magazines as I. Alas, our friendship eventually turned sour.

"Jean-Luc Breton and I (as a co-director) contributed to a very unique review: 'Europe Plurilingue' / 'Plurilingual Europe', which was founded by Nadine Dormoy, a French-American University professor and translator. Breton, an excellent anglicist, also wrote long essays on my work in English—some of it appeared in the prestigious magazine 'World Literature Today',

which is the only review of its kind, anywhere: it publishes essays and reviews in English on contemporary books written in the original language of the author, meaning that all the writers and essayists who contribute to the magazine, are specialized in the literature being written in one or more foreign languages. The review covers literature from the five continents and is connected with the Neustadt International Prize for Literature, whose candidates and jurors—I was one of them—often (25%) receive the Nobel Prize. Breton left 'Plurilingual Europe', because of a tiff with Nadine Dormoy. And since I remained co-editor, he broke up with me too.

"Unlike professional journalists, reporters or essayists, I now seldom write essays. I only take the pen—now I use my computer—when there is a hot topic, whether it is political or literary, which bothers me to a great extent. For instance, when I read or hear blatant lies in the media, or injustices in the literary arena, I get furious and have to put down my opinion on paper. One of my essays on the corrupt French literary prizes, like the Goncourt or the Renaudot, was picked up by The International Herald Tribune (in association with the NYT and the Washington Post) several years ago. I was at once pleased and astonished. But it changed nothing in the French system.

"Adam Donaldson Powell has asked me if my literary archetypes will survive me. He was being magnanimous. I write because it is both existential and therapeutic. But also, in the case of Zapinette, because it is an exorcism. Here, for the first time in my literary life, I began to enjoy myself with all her rants and shenanigans. Zapinette came quite late in my life: 1996. Before that, writing was often painful or an exercise in nostalgia. When I hear some (especially) French authors mention the word 'nostalgia', as if it were a curse, I really have to laugh. She liberated me, for she says things that I couldn't express when I was her age, or that I didn't dare voice later.

"Often young writers come to me with questions, such as: 'Are you happy when you write? Can you give us some tips? What are the main rules for producing a good story, poem or novel? Do you write to be successful and to become a bestselling author?' And the question that used to irk me, even if the intention was benevolent, is 'How many books have you sold?' I now answer in this manner: 'Do you read the 'great' Harlequin books, which sell millions of copies?' Then, no further comment has to be added. I can understand that aspiring writers need mentors and rules. But, since I am not a professor of literature—even though I read regularly in five languages—I have only one

thing to tell them: 'Be sincere when you write, write because you need to, not to please others.' And of course, they are frustrated, for I'm not the right person to be asked these questions.

"This being said, yes I would like to have many more readers around the world, in spite of the fact that I have been recognized by many of my worthiest peers, and in spite of having garnered numerous awards, which I deem to be much more valuable than the 'big' prizes like the Goncourt, in France, or the 'Prix Rossel' in Belgium. At least I know that the contests I take part in are honest; and often anonymous. Actually, my biggest literary honor so far has been to be selected by the Neustadt Committee as a juror. When I got this invitation, I wondered who had supported me, for I knew nobody from that institution. I didn't even know the Neustadt existed, for it insists on not being publicized, lest they be swamped by unwanted requests from editors, authors or publishers. I later learned that a few people on that committee had discovered that I was a bilingual writer and that I was being published in literary and small magazines—but also in some famous reviews like Playboy, Cosmopolitan, etc.—around the world. And they had read some of my work in these journals and reviews. I actually saw them in their library. The international jury is composed of ten or twelve writers or professors from around the world, including very famous authors. The week I spent in Oklahoma was exhilarating. By the way, there too, I was considered to be atypical. Whereas the jurors were all mentioned with their respective nationality, I was and still am the only one who appeared as being a citizen of the world (International or intercontinental—I now forget which), with no nationality attached to my name. And that pleased me enormously, for my nationalities are indicated by my various origins and the languages in which I not only write but those I also speak. If I had seven lives like cats are supposed to have, I would learn the 6000-odd languages of the world, plus all the dialects (the DR Congo alone has more than 300 of them, not counting the six major languages of the country, including French, the official one). And then I would not be restricted.

"We all worked very hard, then met in the evening, exhausted but happy, for dinner. The Neustadt International Prize for Literature is a biennial award for literature, which is sponsored by the University of Oklahoma and World Literature Today (its international literary publication). The jury is always different, not like with the Goncourt, where you have the same old people year in and year out and who, furthermore, work at the major publishing houses.

Actually the Goncourt is a publisher's award, not an author's. And what's worse is that it is given only to the three 'maisons les plus prestigieuses': Gallimard, Grasset and Le Seuil, nicknamed 'Galligrasseuil', with maybe a fourth or a fifth 'big' publisher. But they receive—the publishers, that is—the award by turns. One year it's an author from Gallimard, the next one an author from Grasset, and so on. I call them 'Les trois sorcières' (the three witches), when there are hundreds of excellent smaller publishers, whose authors will never ever receive the Prix Goncourt, nor would they dream of getting it. Speaking of la 'Francophonie', it is a Franco-French invention, which excludes every Francophone writer of the five continents who are not associated with and published by the three witches. In other words, no author of Belgium, Switzerland, Quebec, or French-speaking Africa will ever be 'blessed' with the Goncourt.

"I myself have been a juror for the past 35 years, together with people such as Ionesco and Hélène Arwheiler, the former President of the Sorbonne, for the Prix Européen. I accepted that honor, for it is awarded by the ADELF (Association des Ecrivains de langue française) to writers, hailing from the four corners of the world, whether they have published in unheard of outlets in Africa, the French Caribbean, etc. but also by the famous Parisian publishers, such as—yes, indeed—the three witches, meaning that it is the author who is rewarded, not his publisher.

"So, yes, I am extremely proud to have been noticed by these professors of literature working at WLT and for the Neustadt, for they have a 360° vision of what is being written around the world. This to me is my greatest award.

"But like in any 'business'—that is what the 'mega' publishers consider literature to be—isn't it legitimate to wish for commercial success? And, this without selling one's soul to the devil? No, I will never write to suit a publisher's whim, nor would I change my style for a particular reading public; nor am I able to do so. If some of my work finds particular niches, it is because I have written for over forty years, and that some of my stories or novels just happen to fall within certain ranges. But that was never intended."

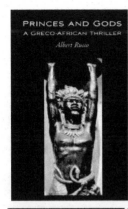

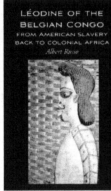

Some of the books by Albert Russo.

Albert Russo on his Flandria bicycle.

Albert Russo receiving the British Diversity Prize in London.

Albert Russo's graduation photo from NYU.

Family photo from South Africa.

PART THREE

ZAPINETTE ON THE LOOSE

A LBERT RUSSO IS USUALLY RATHER SPARSE AND PROTECTIVE AS REGARDS "inside information" about his book characters—including Zapinette, Zaparella, Zapy (amongst her many pet names). Well, all that is about to change, Dear Readers—because I have a very big surprise for you all. But first, let us hear Russo's standard spiel about the Zapinette Series:

"Zapinette lives with her mother, a staunch 'felinist' who owns a beauty parlor in Paris, as well as with Firmin, the latter's boyfriend. The girl however feels much closer to her 'Unky Berky', in spite of the fact that he is "such a weirdo at times and can get on her bloomin nerves". Through Firmin, 'the vermin', she learns that her beloved uncle is a 'homey setchual'. They will travel to many countries together and the trips promise to be quite bumpy, then too, they are peppered with adventures of the quirkiest type."

That marketing blurb is short, alluring and descriptive, without giving all too much away—every publisher's dream. But there is much, much more to both Albert Russo and to his Zapinette Series.

THE AUTHOR'S RESUMÉ OF "GOSH, ZAPINETTE!".

This mammoth volume is billed as "The first ever series of global Jewish humor". While I understand the marketing idea, I see this literary work as much more than that in both scope and content. In my view and experience this book is "a history-of-the-world-in-progress" told by a quirky but witty protagonist with a Jewish heritage. The humorous approach is a seductive mechanism (at times almost propagandistic and at others times almost embarrassingly true) more so than an end in itself. It is seductive because it is endearing enough to entice the reader into following constant and endless paths of thinking perhaps not previously considered. Each of these paths is riddled and spiced with historical, geographical and religious references, anecdotes, allusions to current events, and political commentaries—all weaving a charming and sometimes "wicked" web of associations that are perhaps not always considered to be politically-correct in any one milieu. The author – through the protagonist and "ghost-writer" Zapinette – shoots from the hip in all directions and with aplomb. This book is witty, at times sacrilegious (if not blasphemous), educational and informative, and entertaining. Although almost all of these books have been previously published separately, in this new combined volume the individual books may be experienced and enjoyed as individual stories or chapters (or journal entries) in an ongoing larger set of adventures. This book may be enjoyed as a personalized travel guide and political history "Nouveau Testament", as well as a psychological study of two complementary personas and personalities of the author (Zapinette and her Uncle Berky) and that of the "Contemporary Common Man".

Zapinette is – in my eyes – both a child and an adult. She is the "child in us all" that boldly inquires about and says those things that socially-adjusted and politically-savvy (read "politically-correct") adults may be afraid to say, and/or which we hope will not be noticed or commented on ... be it our appearances, our behavioral idiosyncracies, or politics and events in the world. Her Uncle Berky is more cautious, and is often overrun (and over-ruled) by the more carefree (and perhaps more careless) adolescent who knows and says more than she should. And yet, more often than not, Zapinette is also representative of many values esteemed by representatives of the status quo. She decides herself how to piece together these sometimes competing values within her own illogical but yet logical perspectives on life, humans and world society. Zapinette is always loquacious (except when pouting or suddenly a bit insecure) and oftentimes overbearing and tiring, but she is always true to character: a bit of a true believer cum prophet, and at other times a creative and inquisitive child, and perhaps really just a bystander who is trying to find logical systems of thinking in order to define her own space in the disorderly web of an adult world full of inconsistencies.

The book is written in Albert Russo's signature descriptive style, and although it is well-written and well-constructed the author allows for a degree of haphazardness, some hurried dénouement, the occasional proof-reading inattention, and author-acknowledged repetitions. This lends further to the fun of reading as intentional play with words blend with a refreshing youthful and non-academic style, as well as it keeps the books connected more as stories in this large volume. I suspect that portions of this book are autobiographical (albeit veiled) in personality, perspective and experience, thus giving the reader the added bonus of more insight into a well-known author who has not yet written his formal autobiography. While some readers who are new to the works of Albert Russo may primarily experience the humor in this book, those who are familiar with his African novels and his poetry will recognize both his tongue-in-cheek political commentaries and his occasional passion for ranting about the illogical, the unjust and the plain old "stupidity" he often experiences in our world—both now, and throughout history.

Albert Russo exhibits much courage in publishing this book—both because of its commentary, and also because of his inability not to express his own unadulterated personal truths. I salute and commend his courage and his achievement. I have but one question: when will we get to see "Zapinette – the film"? Anyone in the film industry reading this review?

A WALK DOWN "MEMORY LANE".

Now I think it is time to bring out the biggest surprise of this book: an exclusive interview—featuring Albert Russo, and his heroine Zapinette. But first a trip down "Memory Lane"—revisiting two of their famous episodes.

SCENE FROM ZAPINETTE GOES TO NEW YORK

[CHAPTER XI]

Don't ask what just happened to me. It's so unheard of, it's so ridiculous, I even wondered at first if I was hallucinating, even though I don't smoke pot or sniff crack. I've been kidnapped, I've been goddam kidnapped. We'd had a very late dinner at a TexMex joint with—again! —Mel, Kate and Zac. As we stood in front of our loft, my uncle began to juggle with his bunch of keys—he got tipsy on tequila -, he was taking so much time trying to sort out which was the key to the elevator, which opened the entrance door, that I yelled: "It's freezing, for god's sake. Give them to me, I'll open that damn elevator door." But he was laughing and insisted:

"I have the responsibility, I'm the man of the family, I have to ..."

I would have kicked him in the ass, that's when I'd like to forget I'm his niece, and since I didn't want to be transformed into an ice figure, I decided to go for a jog around the block. I was doing my second round when suddenly I felt a huge hand press against my mouth. I tried to pull it away, but the more I was fighting and thrashing, the tighter was its grip. I remember my nose being so squashed I could hardly breathe. That's when I must have passed out. It's only afterwards that I understood I had been chloroformed, my tongue had such an awful taste.

The following morning, or was it already noon, I woke up, lying on a twin-sized bed within smooth pink satin sheets. A wan light filtered into the room through the curtains, allowing me to distinguish every detail in it. The room was decorated with wallpaper whose printed landscape reminded one of the country, it was full of flowers and mushrooms and hopping bunnies. At least a dozen plush animals lay in an open wicker basket that stood on top of a chest of drawers made of rosewood. It looked like a silent and very orderly menagerie, waiting for someone to enliven it. In a corner, all on its own, sat a panda, almost my size, watching sleepily over his apples and pears.

Then, when I realized I had been abducted, my throat began to knot, but as I surveyed again my surroundings, and recalled the scene of a movie where two children had been taken hostage and shut in a dark cellar, with rats scurrying under their calves, I scolded myself: "Will you cut out the hysterics, already!" So,

I got up in my delicately scented flannel nightie rimmed with dainty little ribbons on the hem and on the sleeves—whoever put this on me had good taste—and walked to the window. Drawing the large veils, I gasped in amazement, for there was Manhattan, unfurling under my gaze as on a giant Miramax screen, with its rows of buildings, its bridges on one side, and its marina on the other, which a thin layer of snow had covered during the night like cake icing.

My stomach was making hungry gurgling sounds when I heard someone knock at the door. I felt my whole body stiffen and couldn't udder a word. The knocking resumed, and as I was still not answering, the door opened slowly. A boy, about my age, came in, accompanied by a very old Chinese couple. He looked only half Chinese, the other half could have been Polynesian or black or latino. I must have appeared as bamboozled as a silly moose, coz none of these three individuals could have abducted me. I stared at their hands, remembering the huge paw that had fallen on my face, nearly making mince meat of it.

The boy stepped forward and held out his hand to me, with these words which, to my enormous surprise, he spoke in French, all bits halting:

"I've been learning French at the bilingual school since I was nine. My name is Charlie-Kea Chang and I'm delighted to meet you. These are my grandparents. They speak very little English, not to mention French, but they too wish to welcome you to our family. If you're here now, it is because of me. My parents and my twin sister died in a car accident last summer, while driving back from Buffalo, New York, where they'd spent a short vacation, visiting with Uncle Chu."

As he was speaking, articulating every word very distinctly, and making short pauses, to be sure I wasn't missing anything, my eyes began to squint dangerously. Then, when I understood why, all of a sudden, my legs seemed to be filling with porridge and my brains with jello, in spite of the fact that I must have slept well over twelve hours. THIS GUY WAS MY SPITTING IMAGE, except that he had a darker skin and—not too overly—slanting eyes. This last realization triggered a series of rabbit farts which I tried to keep silently at bay—not the easiest exercise under the circumstances, you oughta admit. "Well I never," thought I, like my Welsh classmate always says, "not only have I been shanghaied, but I now find that I may also have relatives in Zululand."

139

"It was at Bloomingdale's that I first noticed you." said the boy, with a mischievous twinkle in his eyes. "I was with my grandparents and when I pointed you out to them, the same idea popped in our three minds simultaneously. We then decided to have you followed by Cousin Lee. He's the one who brought you last night to our apartment here on Staten Island. You're my Christmas present."

Listening to Charlie-Kea, I had the impreshun I'd been swept into some comic strip and, instead of getting mad, as I should have, I told him, very pussy mousey:

"But my uncle will worry to death. If he hasn't gone to the police station yet, he's probably inquiring at a number of emergency wards to see whether I wasn't attacked by some lunatic and maybe murdered. Then he will advise my mother and she will kill him."

My comments seemed to have amused the granny and her old hubby, for they were all wrinkles and toothless smiles, even though I'm certain they hadn't a clue of what I was babbling about. Maybe they just thought I was terribly cute or that Snow White had rescoopcitated, sans dwarfs.

"Don't work yourself up like that," said Charlie-Kea, soothingly, "everything will turn out fine, trust me. Cousin Lee went back to the loft, straight after he left you here, and slipped a note under the door, to reassure your uncle, letting him know that you were safe and that you would be looked after like a princess. It also mentioned that you would call him to explain why you are with us— with your consent, of course, for nothing will be done against your will. I believe this note will dissuade him from calling the police. We don't want them in our way, do we?"

Something very strange was happening to me: Charlie-Kea's cuddly ways were turning me into the tamest lil tiger that ever roamed the streets of New York. If he'd been another guy, I would have raised hell and knocked a few of his teeth off, even in front of his granny and his grandpa who kept staring at me, bowing every so often as if to make sure that I got the message. Not in a thousand years would I have imagined that one day I would be standing in front of my double, never mind that he was a boy and half Chinese—and very cute too. I had to pinch myself several times, in different places to prove that I wasn't raving, maybe they thought I had flees or something.

At lunch, the granny served us nems and a variety of dim sum for starters. These were so good, especially the ones filled with ground pork, that I had to have a second helping—I could have just eaten that all the way, but I would have passed for a hillbilly. But when she presented us with a plate of mega prawns which she doused in piping hot tomato sauce and toasted rice, I changed my mind. To please her (and myself) I also had some chicken chop suey . Actually everything tasted so scrumptious, I could have licked not only my chops, but my fingers too. I guess that being a five-star hostage opens your taste buds. For dessert, I had three scoops of ice cream: mango, passion fruit and nutmeg— I was maybe going nuts, but it felt divine.

These folks must have either drugged or hypnotized me, coz I had no desire whatsoever to escape or even to rejoin my uncle— I know, I know, I should feel ashamed to even mention this. The more so, since when I called him, as convened—from a pay phone, you ninny—he whined like an old dog dribbling with remorse, saying he hadn't slept a wink during the night and that he was so relieved to hear my darling lil voice. He stuttered and burped and probably farted too, but the receiver wasn't low enough to get that sound through. He then asked me, after a few hiccups, if they hadn't done anything funny to me. I pretended not to understand and said, "What do you mean, funny things?"

"Well, erm ... they didn't ... erm ... erm ... abuse you, erm... sexually, or any other way." he stammered.

"Oh no," I exclaimed, sounding very innocent, "and in any case, neither Charlie-Kea nor his grandparents have the age for such stupid games." I told him he shouldn't worry at all on account that my hosts were treating me like I was a member of the family.

I even suggested he should enjoy himself and take advantage of all the wonderful things New York had to offer—ok, I sounded like Mayor Giuliani in his preface to The Big Apple Tourist Tips, but you can't always invent your own stuff. "I'll be calling you regularly." I added, to appease him.

Then he wanted to know when I would be back at the loft. At first, I was evasive, but as he kept insisting, I shot back: "Now listen here, if you dare tell my mom about this, something terrible might really happen! She'd get hysterical and wouldn't understand anyway." I felt suddenly very proud to be a hostage and said, full of hutzpa: "It's not like I've been kidnapped for ransom, you won't have to disburse a cent, on the contrary, while I'm staying with these *wonderful people, you'll be able to spare money." That last phrase calmed him down, coz my uncle is a very stingy person. He ahemmed for a while, finding the situation a bit awkward—actually it was very awkward, but I pretended otherwise—and I thought I would give him the works so that he wouldn't bother me anymore with questions. I added a lot of gory details to the story of the accident, saying that not only did Charlie-Kea's folks and his twin sister die in that car accident, but that the poor girl was beheaded and that their cat flew through the window and got harpooned on a fence—I could give Stephen King a few tips for his next movie. I didn't think it necessary to tell him that I was the spitting image of my young host. Goddess knows what would have gone through his already very muddled mind. He stopped being inquisitive and I blew him a kiss through the receiver then hung up.*

With tears in his eyes, Charlie-Kea showed me his family album. The Hawaiian genes came from his mother who had a very round face and a dainty flat nose, with thick jay black hair, like in one of them portraits Gauguin used to paint. She also sported a pair of incredible bazooms, though these weren't out in the air—she would have been arrested for indecent exposure. His father, the Chinese, on the other hand, was wiry as a picket and had in his look something of a horse, on account of his front teeth that jutted forward at least half an inch even when he kept his mouth shut. As for his twin sister, whose name was Pearl, she was quite pretty and wore two long braids that tumbled down almost to her waist. But the strange thing here is that she resembled her brother much less than I do, except that my skin is much pinker. Mystery, Hector'n Tommy, is what I say.

I catch myself suddenly paying more attention to granny and grandpa Chang, and though I'm not the type to slobber over strangers, this new curiosity makes me feel kind of uneasy. Is it because I have never known my own grandparents that I'm being post-mousely nostalgic -'posthumous' smells too much of decay and scares the wits out of me, no one will force me to use it, ok! I've noticed however that this lil ole couple is playing cat and mouse with me, appearing and disappearing like djinns, now together, now one by one. And no matter how silent they remain, I'm no dope. They can grin as much as they wish, creasing even further their eyelids like stoned pussies, it's all writ across their face: "You, lassie, you're going to stay here with us, forever and ever." They'll probably call in a private instructor to give me crash courses in Chinese so that we can start chatting together.

Goddess, what has taken over me, Zaperetta the invertebrat felinist, the worthy successor of Laura McInnerny-Binetti—that's my mother, you ninny— aka Zapi-the-terror, as Unky Berky sometimes refurs to me when he bugs me one time too many and I have to bare my teeth? I've become a computer-robot, recording and taking in everything I hear and see without so much as saying boo. Is this the beginning of Old Timer's disease or have I gotten so lazy upstairs that I'm willingly turning into an oversized marshmallow? What was happening to that darlin' lil French girl who could be so forceful and bold? Would I swap my baguette and my camembert culture for chopsticks, without resisting, like a lame peeping duck?

It's only two and a half days since I've been here and already it seems two and half months, on account that Charlie-Kea is just so adorable. He says I should call him CK—like them men's underwear, which made me blush in the beginning -, and, without asking my permission, he called me Zapie, it's ok, so long as it's not Zaza Chang, Zeech or Zam, coz I would then feel like a real zombie.

CK has introduced me to Chinese Monopoly and taught me checkers and poker—I was never interested in cards before, but with him it's different. He also showed me a number of fantastic conjuring tricks. Jeez that guy is smart and cuuute ... whoa, I can spend hours watching him. I did tell him however that my favorite were video games, there too he is tops. So, on his PC, we tackle Prince of Persia, Mandrake or City Budget, like we were virtual born killers.

This morning we were supposed to go visit the museum at Ellis Island, where millions of immigrants sailed in, but we had to give up because of a snow storm alert. Unlike the French word which sounds as if it has B.O. attached to it, 'Immigrant' in these U.S. of A has kind of a pedigree, especially if your forebears came with the Mayflower—I wonder what your after bears have to say about that. In any case every third Dick and Harriet here hails from some old forsesaken country, even if they got off a raft.

CK seems very proud of his Chinese-Hawaiian heritage. When I asked him if he didn't favor the Yankee side on account that America is the mightiest— dollar- and bang-bangwise -, most awe-inspiring—thanks both to Billy Graham and HollyWoodstock—nation in the world, he said no, that we should all look in the direction of the Pacific and, especially to China, which is not only the oldest civilization there is but that it will soon become Number

One too. I was flummoxed to hear this, coz at first I thought it so great to be a Frenchie who ate Boursin with Beaujolais Nouveau—which the snobs here looove; the non-boozers sip instead lime-flavored Perrier like it was champagne.

After a while, I told him, pussy mousey, that I was also a bit Italian, on my mother's side. If you have some memory left, you'll remember that she had married a US citizen named Brad McInnerny who deserted us to join some topless, flat-nosed hussie in the jungles of the Amazon. So now, here I was, having three different origins.

To my astonishment, CK congratulated me, like I'd just returned from the planet Mars. He then went on, saying that if the Italians cooked the best pasta in the world, it was thanks to Marco Polo who had brought the original recipe from China, and that French cuisine was the most sophisticated in the world ... after the Chinese. So that I shouldn't feel too spare, he admitted that pizza was one of his favorite specialties, with onion soup and crepe suzette. Mentioning all this food gave me hunger pangs.

Thank Goddess, Granny Chang, who is never very far from the scene, reappeared with a plate of kru puk (you oughta pronounce it 'crew pook', not 'puke', you ninny)—them wonderful prawn chips that hug your tongue with nano kisses the moment you open your mouth—with cheese dip and radishes. People in this country, whatever their race or background, love to mix different kinds of foods. 'Hodgepodge' must be an American word, coz this is the only place on this here planet where you can have bits of Frankfurter, turkey and pepperoni on the same pizza, spaghetti with peanut butter, sweet and sour veal parmigian and other combinations I wouldn't dare reveal to the delicate ears of my French compatriots.

There are even restaurants in New York that serve fricasseed snake with bamias in lieu of chicken—go look in the dictionary, you don't expect me to hand you everything on a silver platter, do you?—monkey steaks with celeriac in remoulade—the same here!—and sugar-coated grasshopper crunchies for dessert. Yuck yuck in D major, is what I say.

I forgot to tell you about the aquarium in the livingroom. Though not really big, it has a pretty octogonal form and contains a dozen exotic fishes. Some of them look like living gems, they're so beautiful in their blazing colors, others, with their vivid stripes and geometric designs seem to have come out of the imagination of an avant-garde painter. CK has given each one of them a name and he talks to them as if they were old pals, while stroking their whiskers behind the glass. And you wouldn't believe it, they cling to his fingers in response, especially Pinky and Violetera who flail their tails about, to show how much they enjoy their chat.

This guy, I swear, is super out of the ordinary, coz not only must he have an IQ of 200+—he's skipped two grades at his school, a special institution for over-achievers—but he's probably also endowed with ESP. I'm sure he can read through my mind, coz he never seems surprised by my answers, actually he often precedes them and then it's as if he stole the words out of my mouth, brrr, pretty uncanny. And embarrassing too, for no matter how charming he is, with his cushy slanted eyes and his slick black hair that smells so delicately of lavender, I wouldn't wish him to pry into my inner thoughts. It might give him ideas, like wanting to become a puppeteer, with me as his puppet-in-residence. He claims however that he has found in me his soul mate, his French sister. I'm getting a little bamboozled here, don't forget, I already have a half-brother in Paris, plus this new self-elected one.

To tell you the truth, I felt freer and more respected when I was still a single child, coz the moment lil Peter entered the picture, my mother stopped paying attention to me. Thank goodness I have Unky Berky who does spoil me every once in a while and that I eventually got attached to lil Peter, otherwise I would have had daily fits of jealousy, and jealousy can eat your heart out. With CK, on the other hand, there is no sense of competition, and in spite of the fears I mentioned above, I've never gotten so well with a boy before.

We spent the whole evening surfing on the Web, for CK has virtual pals in the four corners of the world, from Nice to Los Angeles, from Sydney to Honolulu, from Cape Town to Bangkok and who knows, maybe from outer space too. They send each other emails and some of them even have their own homepage which they visit mutually.

He also showed me the official site of Shanghai from where—for you snobs, it's 'whence'—his grandparents hail, saying that they would never recognize their hometown. It's developed so much, it has become the biggest construction site on earth, with triple-decked thruways crisscrossing the city, shopping malls so large you need rollerskates to travel in them, and a skyline that would soon put Manhattan to shame.

You should have seen how his eyes shone when he commented on these feats, clicking on every link available. There were animated clips of the city as it would appear in the near future and previews of fashion shows with some very pretty models.

When I marveled at the fact that the bricklayers seemed to be working nonstop, in day and night shifts, he said it was logical since China had so much to catch up to, after centuries of dormant activity. Well, if you tried to apply this kind of rule to French workers, you might eliminate unemployment, but before that could happen, they would go back and storm the Bastille and tear the new opera house to pieces.

He suddenly turned to me, locking his eyes with mine. I thought I was gonna swoon, expecting some romantic declaration. But to my bafflement, he said:

"In a decade or two, we shall be the rulers of this planet and the West had better behave, including the United States."

I stared at him with my lil weasel pout and stammered, "Fra ... Fra ... France too?"

"Yes," he quipped, with a grin, "even the great land of foie gras will have to watch out and if the European Union doesn't adjust fast, instead of always bragging about its glorious past and shortening its work schedule, you'll be in big trouble."

At once confused and a bit miffed—hadn't he singled me out? -, I retorted, "You ARE an American citizen, aren't you?"

He said of course, but that the only way for the US not to be swept off by this imminent mammoth ground swell, was to combine its forces with those of China, which as its ancient name indicated, was the Land of the Middle.

And for the first time since my abduction I felt tied up, cornered, trapped, for suddenly I recognized that stubborn bulldoggish look of mine imprinted on his face, that look I inflict on my uncle when I see his mind dilly-dallying like a tired old kite. Realizing that maybe he'd shocked me some, CK started smiling again and said, "I'll teach you Mandarin so that one day we might go and visit China together. How about that?"

I just can't switch off this quick and felt like retorting that before I could tackle Mandarin, the fat dudes in Beijing oughta first grant them poor

Tibetans their freedom, instead of letting the Dalai Lama roam the world and tell everybody how badly his people are treated—he's even become a star doing that, earning millions of dollars and garnering an uncushy number of honors from universities and other insitushens of lesser learning.

As I suspected, this guy is a mind reader, coz the next thing he said, to appease or to convince me or both, was that unlike Europe or America, China was a much more homogeneous country and that the few minority problems it had could be dealt with as its economy grew and its population got more prosperous.

Then, without transition, and frowning as gently as he could, —which still meant: you'd better be on my side, orrr else!—he added:

"We will never let anyone take us for a ride again or let them dictate their will like in the times of the International Concessions, at the turn of the century, when the long-nosed imperialists—why was he staring at me now? —sucked the blood of the Chinese people, stoning them with opium, playing one clan against the other and thus spreading anarchy throughout the land. But it wasn't only the English, the Dutch, the French or the Portuguese colonial powers he was blaming. The Yanks too had done terrible things. They had brought to the West Coast, packed in rickety boats, thousands of coolies from Hong Kong and Canton, to build the railroads and toil down the mines. The poor coolies—there certainly was nothing cool about their situation—became so black with soot that you couldn't tell the difference between them and the African slaves who worked by their side. Is that why there are so many Chinese laundry shops in America nowadays? Then, deeming that they were multiplying like rabbits, the government of Uncle Sam banned the Chinese from entering the country altogether.

To prove he wasn't talking through his nose—ok, I admit, it is a wee bit shorter than mine -, CK clicked on the Library of Congress website and showed me how his ancestors were caricatured. It wasn't flattering at all, believe me. There was one picture of a Mandarin dude in traditional garb, wearing a single braid and a pair of satin shoes, busy chomping on a ... live rrrat, with the following caption: "Rid the land of this vermin!" In another drawing, you could see Uncle Sam caught between a bald Chink—their wording, not mine, you ninny!—with an endless pigtail that tumbled down from the back of his head, and a feathered Iroquois. They were both nibbling at Uncle Sam from the opposite extremities. The third one was a photograph of a revolver, surmounted *by a pair of tiny figurines, running after each other, and when you pulled the trigger, the foot of the white hunter was raised, kicking the behind of the robed Chinaman.*

As for the Hawaiians, they hadn't fared much better. Years after the passage of Captain Cook who'd named their area the Sandwich Islands, the Yankee missionaries arrived. The ladder found their beaches so lily white and powdery, their coconuts so luscious and their queen, Cooky Nooky something, so hospitable and complying, that they deposed her at once, creating thus the first pineapple republic in the Pacific—the banana ones came later on. Among other presents, the missionaries brought them their faith and their spirit of enterprise, along with a variety of setchual diseases, known as VD. Then, as they noticed that the locals were dying like flies, they let in the islands droves of coolies from both China and Japan, so that they could cut all that delicious sugar cane that was growing so wildly out in the fields.

According to CK, Hawaiians have invented the sport of surfing, as well as hula hooping—not the cough, you ninny, the dance. I just melt when I see those golden hunks surf on twenty-feet high waves like they were flying fishes.

CK also told me how King Kamehameha ha ha ha—you think I'm making this up? Ok, take away the last three syllables and let's not talk about it anymore—united all the islands under his reign, forming the country as it appears today geographically. He would welcome the pale faced strangers with garlands of frangipani flowers and shell necklaces. So that these foreign dignitaries wouldn't feel too spare during the night—they usually left their wives in the old country to mop the floors and wean their babies—the king would lend them either one of his many wives or of his even more numerous concubines, depending on the rank of these visitors.

No matter how good he may have been to his subjects, that Kameo king would have had his thing twisted to a useless bow tie if he had come face to face with a felinist of my ilk; he would have learnt whose object of whose desire I was, coz such behavior is for the canniballs and the head shrinkers. Apparently the Yankee missionaries, while oohing and aahing in public, promising hell and high water to the heathen, brought back to the continental US some of these customs.

I really don't understand why it's never been the other way round. Look at the bees: not only is the ruler always a queen, but she disposes of her lovers however she wants and, washmore, once they've done their shtick, they conk out. This may be too radical if applied to humans, but if I were the Minister of Education (The French have one and so should the Americans, is what I say) I would force students to study bee culture, and impose as a philosophy theme that they ponder whether to bee nor not to bee. And no further questions asked.

If I were as multiracial as CK, I'd feel like a walking quilt, afraid of losing one of my patches at every toss and turn—and not only in bed, when I have these awful nightmares in which I get chased by rabid bumblebees. As it is, I prefer to forget the boloney side of my family, especially when Unky Berky starts raving in Italian in the middle of the Champs Elysées and people take us for stoopid tourists, or worse, for stranded refugees. CK, on the other hand, is so at ease with all of his different parts that you'd think he was zapping from one nationality to another, like they were TV channels.

He gets as American as apple pie when you broach him onto matters such as science, computers, the Web, video games, and films, featuring Tom Cruise, Schwarzie, Richard Gere, Demi Moore and Kim Bassinger, who are his ideal women—maybe he thinks I'm a combination of these two. Plus Nike sneakers and 501 jeans, among other designer clothes, coz this dude is very fashion conscious and he won't wear just any hand-me-downs . But if you mention swimming and surfing, his Hawaiian genes take over, and does he look luscious with his perennial golden brown tan!

At dinner, when Granny Chang serves us her delicious Peking duck or her beef chow mein, his eyes start glowing with that unmistakable slant. He also points out that a great number, if not the majority, of our consumer goods are now made in China, including Barbetta dolls—I can't stand them, but I don't want to disappoint him, else he takes me for a tomboy -, car and airplane models, most of the electronic gadgets you find on the market, ping pong balls, and so forth and so gong. If they don't stop producing stuff, we'll soon be eating Chinese roquefort with Chabernay from the slopes of the Yangtze Kiang River. I also forgot to mention all the Kung Fu movies he watches.

CK also likes to remind me that the sun rises east of Eden and that China is the most populous entity of our planet, with almost one and a half billion people—he's already included Taiwan and a few other soon-to-be-gobbled territories in this figure. He doesn't say it out loud, but I get the hint: the rest of the world had better keep a low and respectful profile if we don't want to be processed into Purina Chow within the next decade. Even if they never met, Unky Berky thinks exactly like him, isn't that strange and uncanny? Thank Goddess he gets nostalgic every once in a while, coz I'd go crazy staying with a kidnapper who only dealt in pixels 'n stuff or threatened me with the big bad Chinese wolf. He's so much cuter when he waxes poetic and distills names like Mauna Kea, Nuuani Pali, Kahoolawe or Lanai something.

I've gotten so used to CK that I don't even miss Unky Berky anymore—don't go and repeat that, I'd pass for an ungrateful brat. But seriously, I'd better call my uncle as convened lest he think I've been chopped into a thousand pieces and fed to some toothless lion at the Bronx Zoo. Now why have they plonked those poor animals in the city's most dangerous area? I pity them, especially the pink-assed baboons who must be freezing their balls off in this weather.

Talking about monkey business, CK taped a PBS documentary on seahorses and insisted that we watch it together on account that I would learn something concerning evolution. I was flabbyghosted to learn that it isn't the females that bear the eggs in their tummy, but the males. And when they give birth, the babies shoot out of their bodies by the dozens like stray bullets. Then it is the daddy's responsibility to wean his offspring and to protect them against hungry fishes and other predators. What strange lil buggers they are, so tiny and yet so expressive. Actually, they look like a cross between a minuscule mermaid and a minuscule horse, with their head all shrivelled up. And when they gaze at you with their filosofickle mean and their watery eyes, wriggling like tagliatelle that have just slipped out of the pan, they give you the impreshun they're about to disclose some very disturbing secret. I've never seen animalcules this size—I ain't talking of kittens or puppies—that have touched me so deeply. I wonder if the Chinese use seahorses as an ingredient when they cook their delicious fried noodles—poor darling lil souls, that's supposed to be the law of the jungle!

I oughta refrain from blinking like a spastic nerd whenever he opens his mouth, it could give him the wrong impreshun, like I'd do anything to please him, or even be his slave. Something though is happening to me ... I believe ... I am falling ... in love with Charlie-Kea. Now if you don't stop snickering over there, I won't go any further, ok!

As I was saying, the more I look at him, the more my eyelashes flutter, so much so that he asks me whether I feel all right. "Maybe you're coming down with a fever."

"Oh no," I retort, "it must be the New York air. I'm not used to it." or such nannity.

But don't go imagining Goddess knows what disgusting thing, coz what I feel for Charlie-Kea ain't of a setchual order, capish! It's more to do with Master Narcissus who, back in Ancient Greece, fell in love with his own image, reflected in a pond. When I glance at Charlie-Kea from the corner of the eye, I see myself and, darn it, I like what I see. And don't goggle at me like that. He's the one who's triggered the whole thing, remember, when he saw me at Bloomingdale's. He claims that such happenings aren't at all coincidental—they're supposed to be all written down for us, even if we had no clue beforehand—and that it would be a shame, nay, a crime, to let such occasions pass by. It's like a cloud of golden nuggets breaking all of a sudden over your garden and you just have to pick them up.

Nevertheless, kidnapping a young girl in a foreign country, without any warning, is a bit thick, you oughta admit. And wash more, I don't even know what Cousin Lee, my abductor, looks like, he must have doused me with tons of chloroform. I wonder what kind of activities he performs in Chinatown. He may be an appointed killer or even a clan don. I just hope he doesn't deal in hard drugs and sell them to kids—if he did that, I'd bash the daylights out of him the next time we meet.

Since I came here, my mind has been racing like a mad dervish. I'd better put some restraint on such wild guesses. Maybe I should have listened to Unky Berky and not forced him to show me all those video cassettes, marked PG.

"They're much too violent for a little girl of your age." he'd whine, but I would just shrug my shoulders, calling him a sissy, specially after we'd seen The Rock , with Sean Connery. There were a few ketchup scenes and in the middle of the movie, he had to excuse himself. He stayed in the bathroom a quarter of an hour. When I think that he wanted to become a doctor! He would have puked over his patients every time he'd have had to perform surgery.

I have a slight inkling I'm being brainwashed, but CK is such a darling I can't possibly get mad at him. That sounds like the reaction of a wimp, hey, don't stare at me!

He claims that much of Western technology derives from China and that I shouldn't heed all the slogans our scientists pour out. While the Gallic tribes were fighting each other with arrows and hunting warthogs for their supper, the

Chinese were concocting things. To give me the proof of the pudding, CK drew up a dazzling list. Chess, paper money, matches, playing cards, gunpowder, fireworks, kites, watches, umbrellas, the printing press, and even whiskey, which everyone thinks is Scottish, were Chinese inventions. They were also the forerunners in astronomy, in maths and in medicine.

Apparently the French were not the first to have discovered the decimal system. Guess who? Poor Monsieur Mètre, he must be turning in his grave at the Père Lachaise cemetery. Would you believe too that fluorescent paint originated in China, on account that some insomniac found a silkworm in the middle of the night that was all lit up from the inside, to ward off the spirits of darkness?

Blood circulation was another one of their discoveries; before that people probably believed that humans functioned with gas, which came out as farts.

If you thought kites were a harmless device, you're wrong. They were used in the Middle Kingdom as propaganda leaflets in times of war. The army generals would send them out either to mislead their foes or to warn their allies of the next attack.

I didn't want to offend Charlie-Kea, but his list failed to mention a number of lesser inventions, like water dripping, the pulling of nails, the tickling of feet and other little tortures used as means of persuasion. The Japanese have perfected these during WWII, applying them to their POW.

Sfars ballistic state-of-the-art is concerned, CK told me that the famous Exocet missiles the Americans showered Irak with during the Gulf War had a 14th century AD Chinese precursor, named 'Dragon Flames'. He also showed me a piece of medieval artillery called 'Thunderclap Fire Thrower'. The ladder would launch smoke bombs made with the most disgusting ingredients. When CK realized what they were all about he quickly clicked on the Return button, but I'm just as fast as he is and I also read the contents. There was gunpowder, of course, arsenic—no old lace though -, mixed with human turd that has been dried out and sifted, aconite, which is supposed to be some kind of monkey's hood, croton oil—a very potent laxative -, pellets of squashed blow-flies, yellow wax, tinted with witch piss and other stuff whose composition I skipped but which stank worse than everything else. These ingredients were mashed and subsequently boiled to form compact masses.

The Chinese also produced a cannon dubbed 'Sprinkler of Magic Mist', which is a pretty description for launching diarrhea bombs ... yuck ... yuck ... triple yuck. But that's not all, they also invented ballistic fans that spread this unmentionable stuff around. I bet you didn't know the expreshun "when the shit hit the fan" came from there.

Right after that, thank Goddess, Charlie-Kea found, always on the Web, a toy section with life-size models that dated back to the 4th century AD. Like this dragonfly carved in bamboo which had an axle with a small cord around it and tiny blades set on its sides. You just had to pull the cord and the dragonfly would rise and perch aloft a tree or wherever you destined it to go. It was only in 1800 and something that George Cayley, an English engineer, who was also a pioneer of modern aviation, discovered the toy and thought of building a helicopter.

CK also claims that Leonardo da Vinci whose Mona Lisa was really a dragabushkin and not at all an expectant mother, notwithstanding her angelic smile, copied the Chinese in most of his so-called discoveries. Ditto for the parachute, the helium-filled balloon and the sailing board them Californian hunks flex their muscles on to impress the girls—and the homeys too.

As for hell's bells—them that ring in Christian churches and give me bloomin' headaches -, they already existed in China five centuries before the birth of Christ. Come on now, would he have me believe that the space shuttle is a butterfly dinosaur that went cosmic, just with a few micro chips added to it? And that the French TGV—the bullet train, you ninny—was just a farting caterpillar, also invented originally in the times of Mathusalem? I'd say, without being overcritical, that my young protector is a wee bit chauvinistic on the Chinese side. In spite of that, I think he's the most gorgeous, most brilliant, most enlightened guy on earth. I feel so much under his spell that I consider him my guru. Is that the effect of love? Feeling weak at the knees, when you least expect it, and taking as gospel every word that comes out of the horse's mouth—hey careful, here, it's just an expreshun, I never said CK was a horse, ok -, even when he goes round the bend, asserting things not even Mao Ding Dong would have believed?

I get hot flushes all over my body and my eardrums are abuzz with sweet whispers whereas he stays as cool as a cool cat and continues to treat me like his kid sister.

What must poor Pearl be thinking from up there, stranded in her corner of Paradise and surrounded by chunky lil Buddhas? I would die of jealousy if I were her, even if she can't die a second time. Talking about souls and stuff, I loved Whoopi Goldberg in the movie Ghost where she played the clairvoyant, trying to communicate in the hereafter with Patrick Swayze who, she learns, hasn't died at all accidentally but was murdered by a colleague of his.

Maybe Pearl and I would could become friends instead of rivals, but how can I get in touch with her? It would seem too lewd-i-crass for words if I wrote to Whoopi, c/° her agent, and request her to be our go-between—in any case those agents throw most of the fan mail, including expensive presents, down the bin, coz I've written to some of my favorite stars and never got any response. I thought of suing them for mental cruelty and heartless indifference, after all, without us, admirers, they'd all be on the dole.

When I think of it, I'm a very consenting hostage, my oh my, and if I weren't that nice, I'd blame my uncle for it, on account that he took so much time to open the door locks. I wouldn't have trotted around the block in that freezing weather, and Cousin Lee wouldn't have been able to catch me.

In the olden days, when I used to hear about terrorists kidnapping children, I wished the cops would get them, or worse that they'd be 'accidentally killed'—that's called 'virtual suicide'. It always seemed a mystery to me that some victims, after a while, would sympathize with their abductors, and in some cases even got friendly with them. I was certain they were acting under pressure, either because they got drugged or were hypnotized, coz to be so forgiving ain't normal. Well, I can assure you I'm perfectly sober and I don't wish for a moment to denounce Charlie-Kea or his grandparents, even if the ladder keep staring at me for hours like a pair of grinning pekinese. But then, as if the instinct of self preservation was stronger than my feelings, I said to myself: "Who could ever have imagined that one day I'd be sitting here with these Chinks. Wow!" The dirty word escaped me again and at that very moment Charlie-Kea locked his eyes with mine in a most magnetic fashion, as if to mean: "Don't worry, dear, I'll rid you of all the bad vibes still lurking inside your little head. I'm your guardian angel, remember."

Then, as if on cue, I asked myself if 'Amerloque', which the French use whenever Uncle Sam flexes his muscles, was a worse insult than 'Chink' or 'Yid' or 'Nigger'.

154

And you won't believe it, Charlie-Kea nodded yes, putting a finger across his lips. It gave me the willies, like when I watch some of the scarier episodes of the X-Files.

I'm not sure whether what follows is a dream or whether I have entered Luc Besson's Fifth Dimension —it's the title of a movie, Mr. Ignoramus! Anyway, this is what happened. Charlie Kea took me to an athletic club somewhere in Chinatown. And there, for the first time in my life, I saw Cousin Lee, my kidnapper. He was making Kung Fu passes at some younger guys. He was probably their coach. Gosh what a hunk that dude was, not my type, but a hunk nevertheless! You should have seen his pecs, his arms, and the size of his thighs, muscles rippling like he'd just slipped out of a jacuzzi filled with olive oil. A real ox. After a while, he began to measure himself up with adults and he would twist their limbs like they were sausages or liquorice, then make them whirl like helpless kittens. I wondered how his poor victims could still be in one piece, after being hurled to the other side of the room so brutally, and I'm talking of beefcakes, not wimps. He probably learnt a few tricks from Jean-Claude Vandamme. Thank Goddess Unky Berky wasn't around when Cousin Lee took me away, he would have been reduced to an omelet—sans mushrooms.

After the match, Cousin Lee walked straight towards me and gave me a hug, while he lifted me in the air like I was a feather. "Hi Cousin Zapinette!" he groaned, baring his frightfully gleaming teeth. I was overwhelmed, as much by his strength as by his big brother bear gentleness. We then all went to his restaurant—Cousin Lee is also a chef.

As I began to dig into my deliciously crisp Peking duck, the entrance door flew open, letting in two cops, followed by ... Unky Berky, Kate and Zac.

"Hands up, everybody!" hollered the fatter of the two, aiming his gun in our direction. At that very second, I felt Cousin Lee's arm press hard against my chest in a shield. The other cop approached us stealthily from the opposite side, and, I can't tell how, but Cousin Lee, through one of his Kung Fu tricks, managed to send him rolling back all the way to where his colleague stood, all the while he kept me locked against his arm.

The fat cop lost his balance as well as his gun. But before Cousin Lee could get hold of the pistol, three other cops burst into the restaurant. And minutes later, my poor kidnapper had his hands cuffed. But when they also arrested Granny and Grandpa Chang and my lover boy, I yelled:

155

"Leave them alone! These people haven't done anything wrong." and, doing my Joan of Ark shtick, I added, "You put them in jail, I go with them. I refuse to be separated from my family."

Unky Berky couldn't believe his eyes, neither could Zac, though Kate winked at me conspiratorially, to show her felinist solidarity.

During the trial, I kept hammering in that they were my American-Hawaiian-Chinese family and that my name from now on would be Esmeralda McInnerny-Chang. They wanted proof? They just had to look at both Charlie-Kea and me, unless they were blind. Since they couldn't deny our uncanny resemblance, we were all acquitted. The judge did try to dilly-dally, pointing out that we didn't have the same complexion or the same shape of eyes. But I shut him up calling him a racist. Of course, I never so much as hinted that I had fallen in love with CK and that I planned to marry him in the future, but that's between you and me, coz such a revelation would have messed up the whole caboodle. What bothers me though is that my lover boy has no clue about this. I will just have to be patient and learn from Granny Chang some Oriental wisdom—even if at times she drives me round the bend with her cushy bows and slanted smiles.

In literoity-toyty terms, I'm writing the epilogue here. But this is only the beginning of something else and if I don't get Old Timer's disease precociously, you will hear from me again soon.

When we flew back to Paris, me and my uncle, and told my mom about the Changs, she almost freaked out. "What!" she exclaimed, "You with Chinks! Isn't it enough that they're invading the world with their food and their wares? Now you want to impose them on us."

I tried to bring her to reason, with the—not very convincing—help of Unky Berky—on account that his mind is still full of Zac, his collages and whatnots.

The evening of our arrival, I called Charlie-Kea, reversed charges, to prove to my mom how generous he was, and when I passed him on to her, hearing him speak in French, she remained stunned. After that brief conversation—she did manage to say "erm … erm …" a few times -, I informed her that I intended to learn Mandarin on account that China would be the Superpower of the new century and that if she didn't too, she'd be left out. She was too bamboozled to answer. And I immialtely put forth to her the blueprint of my theory of economic and cultural union between the EU, the US and China, which I insisted was essential to our survival. This all probably sounded like raving diplomacy to her, but with the wisdom of Granny Chang slowly rubbing off on me, I have no doubt she will soon adhere to my new philosophy.

If you want to know what happens next, you will have to wait till I write a sequel. In the meantime, Charlie-Kea says hello.

～☙❧～

SCENE FROM ZAPINETTE BURQA BURQUETTE

[CHAPTER SIX]

Fatiha came to me crying her eyes out. That poor girl really fatigues me with her family's catastrofickly goings-on. From now on I'll call her Fatiga, coz it's ok to have compassion, but at the end of the day, if there's too much of it, it compresses your heart and turns it into a piece of mush, then you want to bring up! Wow, compassion demands a lot of strength and courage, I don't know how long I'll be able to be com-passssio-nate. I'd rather listen to that old Cuban band Compay Segundo, them gagageniarian musicians with no teeth left but with a lot of dancing rythm.

Ok, now to the new disaster that has just plagued Fatiga's folks. She has an aunt, just a couple of years older than herself (she ... she ... shit), can you imagine! How do you figure having an auntie or an uncle almost your age? Well it apparently often happens in Muslim families, when your own grown-up uncle marries a girl (his third or fourth wife) of fourteen! In this case, her auntie Amina who is thirteen and a half and who was born here in France, was forced by her parents—who in reality are Fatiga's grandparents, do you follow me? Don't bother, I hardly follow it myself, it's too damn complicated for our poor Western brains—to go to Algeria, where she's never set foot before, and marry someone quadruple her age. Amina first thought it was a joke, but when her father hollered at her and threatened to flog the heck out of her buttocks, she understood that he was damn serious. So, during her summer vacations, Amina

157

*and her folks flew to Oran (not orang utan, you geographic nerd, that's a city),
she saw nothing of the town and even less of its lovely beach. No, they all went
from one house to another, drinking mint tea, eating shawarma, couscous, and
delicious other home-cooked tidbits, with syrupy desserts full of honey and
sesame and so fork and ding dong. But a fat lot poor Amina enjoyed all them
goodies, cooked to honor her and her parents. The bozo she was to marry was a
rich farmer, who owned two dozen goats and thirty sheep, he himself was the
size of a hippo, with a mouth that seemed to have been repaired by a plastic
surgeon, so balthazarish his thick lips were—you'd have thought that behind
them he had maybe three tongues, coz he ate like a pig. By the way, you do
know that Muslims aren't allowed to eat pork, it's haram, totally forbidden, on
account that it isn't hallal—by now you must be familiar with all these words,
I've spelled them enough times, so pay attention, ok.*

*So, Amina returned from that first trip to North Africa depressed, deflated—
she ate hardly nothing, she just couldn't swallow what her folks had prepared for
her, the future marriage with Salaam el Pigo, I mean, and consequently, her
throat closed up, refusing anything that oughta have passed through it, except
for liquids; she drank so much that she spent a third of her time there, peeing,
which was the only relief left to her, at least in the loo no one was ogling or
leering at her nearly inexistant tits—and totally dejected, actually she felt that
her own soul had been ejected from her body and she couldn't recognize herself
when she faced the mirror. 'Who's that person in front of me,' she would ask
herself, 'a servant, a slave, a Mamelukette' (ok, that's me adding)? She dreamed
of being completely engulfed in a nikab, with just the eyelashes sprouting out
from the tiny cotton cleft, like some mustacho bristle, and divided in two,
washmore, where the nose stands—in such cases, not even the nose is to be seen,
can you imagine, as if it were a phallinozick symbol; I don't know if you
remember that jerkette of an aristocritic girl, classmate ha!—who always wants
to be my best friend in order to share with me all the nasty things she thinks of
everybody else, on account that she's the opposite of a beauty, more the crossing of
an opossum and a baby croc, with on top of it, a face so pockmarked, you'd
swear an army of ants visits her every night. Yeah, according to her, boys who
have big schnozzles have a big thing down there. What about her, coz not only
are her nasal flippers narrow, but they are the size of a worn out shoehorn and
they're as bent as a crows's beak, with so many holes in it that you'd think it was
at the lowest rung of the pecking order. Now DO you remember her? Charlotte
de Jerk, the one who believes her ancestor was Louis the Fourteenth's commode*

guard, in other word, the guy who brought HRH ('his royal highness', for you nerds!) the wooden thingamagig with a hole carved in the most precious rosewood for the royal number two, and if that wasn't enough, the guard had to be present while Louis was pushing down, full force and full stink, and make sure it was nice and big so's to show the doctor the stuff for the ladder to see and smell if everything was norrrmal, fercryinoutloud!—nowadays, thank goddess, at least here in the West, we have proper WCs. Apparently the Japanese have even invented one that sprinkles your tushy then wipes you off with jets of hot air so that you can dispense with regular toilet paper.

Even back in France, Amina refused to eat, and she became anorexitically thin, to the point where you could count her ribs—they were probably tickling her to death -, my oh my, I wouldn't want to see a sight like that, it's concentration camp stuff.

Her parents took her back to Algeria during the Christmas vacations (it's Catholic, not Muslim, you nerds), and it all resumed like in the previous summer, only now the weather was cooler and she continued to sweat, not because of the heat, mind you, but because of her nerves being all twisted and contorted, with her mind going bonkers. Isn't the human body stupidly constructed? you get hot even when there's a cold breeze around you and you shiver, fercryinoutloud!

If we are made in the image of God, then He must have stopped working on mankind early on, maybe regretting that He ever started the whole caboodle. He probably intended to massproduce us, instead of acting as the craftsman he ought to have been. Just compare them made-in-China slippers and bespoke (yeah, shake'em pears again) hand-sewn babouches (them beautiful leather flip flops you can buy in a Moroccan market—they're so genuine, they still stink of bleeting goats, having just taken their crap, you know them tiny balls that look like playing marbles, only that in this instance, they're mushy and dark brown. I can see Him—God in Hell—yawning out of boredom when He got to the tenth of his job, saying to Himself: «Let those unfinished humans cope with what I gave them, shiiit, who do they think I am!»

Actually, I'm doing him a damn favor by refurring to him with a capital h. he doesn't deserve it, naaah, even if the h stands at the beginning of a sentence.

Had we been 'manufactured' by a Goddess, I'm sure, we would be in a much better shape, on account that women are more finicky and they usually like things well done, look at most of the housewives around the globe. What would their hubbies and children say if they gave them rotten food to eat, with cockroaches or strands of hair floating in the soup, and if they kept the bathroom disgusting and smelly, not to mention bedsheets full of lice or whatnot—yuk yuk and double phew.

Yeah, that god with his bloomin beard makes me think of today's ISIS and Al Qaeda monsters with their Kishkas-nikovs hanging on their shoulders as if they had been born with them. They looove to film children wearing them too, with the difference that the Kishkas-nikovs are bigger than the kids themselves. Nice example they give them. 'Kill, kill, maim, maim' is their motto and don't you confuse it with Rita Hayworth's song 'Put the blame on Mame', when she dances like a gypsy queen in that mafioso nightclub, making her lover's blood boil, ok! That's an entirely different story. It's called unrequited love, meaning: «I love you yeah, I love you not, I dunno if I really love you, so, to hell and gone.» And it all ends with passionate murder and sobs and mumblings «Oh why did I do it, why ... why, and so fork and dingdong.» and this is supposed to be god's masterpizza? Pizzas are some of my favorite dishes, specially when they are crusty and thin like the real Eyetalians cook them 'al forno'. Quiet now, Shushsh, let me go further with Amina.

Back in Algeria, around Christmat time, Amina's fatso fiancé gave her the most magnificent jewels she ever saw: an emerald engagement ring set in red gold, with lil diamonds surrounding the big stone—don't forget that green is the color of Islam—along with a matching necklace and a bracelet, both in the same precious red gold, studded with dozens of small emeralds and tiny diamonds—not Swarovsky, you nerd, those are much less expensive.

Her parents almost jumped out of their skins for joy. I just can't imagine who invented that stoopid expreshun, how can you jump out of your body and remain whole? unless you've already become a ghost. But Amina plunged inside her own skin, if you want to go on with that expreshun, meaning that her cheeks got swallowed inwards, her eyes became smaller than ever and her bosom stretched to that of a boy, not to mention the rest of her, which floated puppetlike within her clothes while her head disappeared behind her veil, so that you could only see her nose jutting out, like a very wrinkled finger.

Gosh, she must have looked worse than the shadow of E.Tette (the feminine of E.T., if you haven't understood it). Then, all of a sudden, roboticwise, her face swung left then right, right then left, and so fork and ding dong, for five solid minutes that must have seemed like a whole hour—try to watch a movie scene getting jammed because the damn projectionist, instead of following the film for which he is responsible, takes a snooze and spectators have to wait till he wakes up.

Amina's parents, her fatso fiancé and his family—parents, brothers, sisters, aunties, uncles, cousins and even dogs and cats—watched her aghast, yeah yeah, she was more of a ghost at that moment rather than flesh and bone.

«What's wrong, darling?» Amina's mother asked her, getting brown-purple.

Amina opened her mouth but no words came out, only a hiss like Serpentina, in a Walt Disney animated toon.

Fatso's parents also got very worried and brought back some resurrecting salts from the bathroom then sprayed them on the poor girl's face all the while an old toothless aunt waved a fan at her, made of dry camel skin, before she would faint or even suffocate and stop breathing altogether. But all to no avail, on account that Amina felt even worse and thought her last second was near ('last hour' is much too long in cases like this).

She was laid on Fatso's parents' bed—a mega-mouse-size piece of furniture surmounted by a velvet-covered canopy, with its four spiral-bound poles painted in blood red; maybe they thought that that bullish color would give the poor girl a healthier look, coz you should know that in those developing nations supertissues (superstition, ha!) go hand in hand with modern stuff like Kleenex and microwaves. Have you ever watched some of the Saudi camel drivers, holding a cell phone close to their ear and wearing Nikes?

When Amina came to (to what? that's an expreshun), she must have believed she was wandering in a fairy tale, until ... until she recognized Pigface. Then, all her screws went bang and, for the first time since she'd arrived in Algeria, she started hollering:

«I don't want to get married. No one has asked my opinion. Go to hell all of you!»

My oh my! The scandal that ensued shook the whole house as if a bomb had just exploded. Usually, when Muslim women celebrate a happy occurrence, like an engagement party or a wedding, they let out loud youyous, lolling their tongues in every which way, while clapping their hands so hard that some of them brake a few fingers. But in this case, instead of youyous, the attending

161

females, young and old—there might have been a dozen of them around, not counting Amina's mother—made high-pitched bleating noises like pregnant nanny goats that are pushing to give birth but can't, for some reason or other. At a certain point, Amina thought she was going to drown in a pool of spit they were spewing so much saliva on her. The men, on the other hand, or better said, on the other caboodle, groaned like a herd of warthogs.

In spite of all the racket, or maybe, encouraged by it, the girl got up from the bed and ran away into the streets of Oran.

They had to call the police, describing Amina like someone who had just escaped a madhouse, and low and bee bold, half an hour later, they found her and returned the girl, whose dress was in tatters, as if she had been manhandled or maybe worse—she did look like a little slut—all black and blue, manacled and gagged with a one of them Palestinian chèches (shawls, you nerd). If anyone dared do something like this to me I would kill him, I swear, I would KILL HIM, but by first crushing his kishkes with the heaviest pan I could find in my kitchen. And you think I am being vulgar? Who is the vulgarest in this situation? I ask you—no, I refuse to ask you, if you don't agree with me, you're no better than a stinking hyena. This is the age of felinists, enough with the MCPs already—oh, you still need a translation? Male Chauvinist Pig, like Pigface who thinks he can have Amina at his beggaring call.

The worst of all was, after Amina got back to the livingroom, washed and dressed in pajamas, her mother and Pigface's mom, asked all the men to get out, on account that they wanted to make sure she was still a virgin. A VIRGIN, FERCHRISSAKE! after what the police did to her! The girl was then uncushily ordered to pull down her pajamas and to open her legs, like some cow ready to be milked. Then, one after the other, the two moms fiddled with her thing and while Amina was shaking with sobs, for which they couldn't care less, they both sighed in unison, like two bloomin crackling loudspeakers, full of static:

«She's intact, she's intact, oh Allah be praised, Allah be praised a thousand times.»

They felt so elated, that they embrassed each other, drooling on each other's cheeks and peeing for joy like two old incontinent bitches, guffawing when they realized they were all wet thereunder, and as they left the room, they pressed their hands hard over their mouths to try to muffle their outbursts, all of this, without nary (shak'em pears word) a look at the girl, who lay there as if she had become an inflatable doll that someone had left behind, with the difference that it was a crying doll— the Japanese, who are experts in creating ersatzky humans and robodogs, have even invented artificial tears (you just have to press a tiny button at the back of the doll's head and there you are).

Both families looked radiant, while Pigface got so delirious that he flew to the jeweller's and scampered back with a brooch in the form of a crescent, inlaid with emeralds, of course and, underlined by a string of dainty little rubies.

He presented the pretty blue box, knotted with a red velvet ribbon to 'my most adorable fiancée'—yeah, Amina became very adorababble the moment he learned she was still a virgin, this being reconfirmed at least two dozen times by who you know, in case the others, specially the men, had hearing problems. «Could you repeat that again?»

The 'adorabbbable' girl was sitting between the two moms, who looked like two guardian bulldogesses, on the livingroom settee, totally blank and as white as her dress and her veil—she looked pathologically married already, yet had no clue of what was happening to her. Actually she had become catatonic (not canonical, you nerd), it means that your heart and your eyes get so catastrofickly intertwined that you don't know whether you are coming or going, where? That's the unanswered question, specially when like in this case, youre staying put. Just imagine, riding a roller-coaster, while you're stuck to your WC seat. Well, that's how Amina felt.

As she continued to look blank, her mom, who suddenly remembered she had a daughter, mumbled sweetly at her: «Open it, deary, it's for you.»

But as the girl wasn't budging and floated in Catatonia, her mom untied the velvet knot then, discovering what was inside the box, exclaimed:

«Amina, Amiiina, daaarling—now she was her darling, yeah, but a little girl could say the same thing to her rubber doll—do you realize how magnificent this gift is? And it is from your future husband!»

163

The last word had the effect of an electric shock—you know, like the ones skyatrysts administer their demented precox patients, in order to revive their hibernating cells -, and Amina shot up on her two flimsy legs then ran to her room, screaming:

«Never, neeeever, I willl never get married to him.»

After that scene, both families agreed that the girl should go back to France and rest for a while, before her parents tried to convince her again to reconsider.

So, Amina went to the seaside with her folks, who were now afraid to speak to her, on account that she had the look of a scrawny tigress who had lost tufts of her coat and would do anything to sink her claws onto the next passing prey, the prey being, here, either of her parents.

«How long will she be like that? I'm fed up,» the father whispered to his wife.

«She needs to let off steam, be patient, Abdallah, she will eventually come to reason» the mom said suavely to her nervous hubby who was fidgeting between the bedsheets like a caged lion.

But when, instead of sending Amina back to school in September, as she was expected to, her parents planned a third trip to Algeria, the girl got wild, ran out of the apartment and disappeared for a few days. Her family summoned the police and the search began, feverishly. The mother cried her eyes out, so much so, that her hubby, who couldn't stand it any more beat her like hell and broke her nose.

On the sixth day—hey, god was supposed to have finished his creations, before the sabbath, during which everybody had to stop working and enjoy life -, the gruesome conclusion was revealed: Amina had hanged herself in the attic of a schoolmate's apartment, two kilometers away from her folks'.

This kind of story gives me the willies, inasmuch as it is a true one. How can a family behave that way with their children? It is crimmmminnnal.

But wait till you hear the last straw. Amina's parents went with the whole family to their deceased daughter's school and asked the

Headmistress if her class could spend a day off to mourn the girl. They would offer each one of them almond cookies with sesame.

By now, of course, the whole school had learnt about the story, from hearsay, as well as through the local and the national media. Furious, the Headmistress shot daggers at them, flared up, with the nastiest look she ever gave anyone, and screamed:

«What cheek! Get out of here, YOU HAVE KILLED YOUR OWN DAUGHTER.»

—⌀⌀—

A SURPRISE INTERVIEW!

Adam: Well, Albert and Zapinette—that was exhilarating! You have quite a way of describing things—both in detail and as a confluent finger painting, but with color splashing and spattering everywhere. Could you both tell our readers a bit about how you work together to create these books? Zapinette, I assume that Albert (your Uncle Berky) probably has to structure all of these stories into a book format that his publishers will agree to sell, but you seem to have the best insight into how things that are happening in front of your eyes relate to other things happening (or which have already happened) in the world. And you might have better computer skills than him. Or do you talk through all the things and ideas in the books, and then start writing? Do you sometimes feel like a voice in Albert's head, Zapinette? Like his alter ego, perhaps?

Zapinette: Alter ego, alter nothing, I'm the alter of nobody. I'm unadulterated. I didn't say I'm an adult, you ninny, it means I'm pure me, I and myself, capish! Yeah, I was born from the fig of Albert's twisted imagination—strange how a mushy brain can cough up some gems; it's like them blood diamonds you find in the Congo; and now I'm flying with my own wings and swim with my own gills. I already have more than enough on my

165

hands with Unky Berky—ok, true, I can't live without him, in spite of his shenanigans; it's a full time job, and I go to school, washmore. An ass-side: hey Adam did you clean your teeth? I can smell beer and sauerkraut. As for Albert, he can go to pot, don't be vulgar, I didn't say that he has to sit on a potty all day long.

Albert: One day in 1996, I felt so miserable, I told myself: enough already. I had a hero named Ripov, but he was a loser and that was getting on my nerves. I needed something uplifting, and so, out of the blue came Zapinette, with all her quirks and her tantrums. Thanks to her I could redesign a new childhood, replacing mine which was quite depressing. She dared say and do all the things I was afraid to do and say, because I was so shy and so helpless, until I started high-school. I let Zapinette be, and as it was mentioned before, there isn't much of a plot in her books, and though it can sometimes be tricky, I try to put some order in her verbal diarrhea—just don't tell her I used that last word, she would throw a brick at me, or worse.

Adam: Albert, when exactly was Zapinette born? Has she ever personally met any of your other characters (excuse me, Zapinette—I mean "Stars") such as Ripov? Is it possible that Zapinette and Ripov will perform together in a future novel? And you, Zapinette—how would you feel about sharing your "main character" role and voice with another?

Zapinette: I won't share anything with nobody, you're joking or what! Ripov is a silly goose who can't defend himself. I already have to take care of my uncle, isn't that enough? Berky writes Ripov stories, to vent his frustrations, but my uncle ain't stupid, he forces me to study all the bullshit you have to know about a country before we take a trip, and washmore, to deliver a written report on what we have visited, ten forks and ding dong. Then too, I have to accompany Monsieur Binetti to museums, to artsy fartsy galleries, and even to operas, fercryinoutloud, otherwise we can't go to the movies of my choice or buy nifty sweaters, hip shoezzies and trinkets—oh I just looove costume jewellery and miniatures of animals, dinosaurs and stuff—for Bibi (that's cutie pie lil me in Frog talk). Yeah even my teacher says I'm kind of pretty, but I have a problem with her, on account that she's enamoured of me, and makes incredibly big doe's eyes at me in the middle of a lesson, even when I don't have to answer questions—yeah in this here specific case doe can be chucked in with do's and don'ts, and it's certainly a don't, coz I ain't no setchual pervert. Can you believe that crap?

Albert: I said that already, though I have to add this. After I wrote Zapinette Video, which became quite popular, readers asked me if there was a sequel. I had no intention of doing that. But then my French publisher asked me to oblige. Actually, I have to thank them for my continuous trek with Zapinette, because I owe my sanity to her. I only realized that once I planned to take her around the world and to live the wildest and zaniest adventures of her life.

Adam: You both love to travel, and you have been to many countries already. Do you have new travel adventures planned for the near future? If so, then where to? Where would you most like to travel to next, Zapinette—and why? Are there places you would refuse to visit? And please tell us why?

Zapinette: Oooh, now that I have caught the travel bug, I couldn't go back to like when I was little. My uncle and I have become globetrotters emeritus— that's Latin, and I don't know if it fits here, never mind. Yeah, I want him to take me to the anti- and the phily-podes. Oh, so it doesn't exist! Well now it does. Who is the writer? Everywhere, except them countries where they beat women and use their wives as servants or worse; them where they have to wear chadors and burqas, you know, where they look like black ghosts or walking mailboxes.

Albert: Zapinette and her uncle follow my steps: they visit every country I have had the privilege of discovering.

Adam: Zapinette, you are a very mature young woman—sometimes you seem to understand more of the ways of the world than your Uncle Berky. How does such an intelligent woman as you get along with other youngsters your own age—such as at school? Not everyone is as smart as you or Charlie-Kea. Are you popular with other girls at school? Describe your current best friends. What "survival advice" do you have for other young women your age who are like you? And Albert, you are very studious and self-disciplined. Many of your main characters seem to have inherited similar qualities. Do you easily suffer people you consider to be ignorant and lazy?

Zapinette: I suppose I owe my sofisticle education to Unky Berky, on account that whether I want to or not, I have to read stuff that can be as heavy as lead, like a brief history of the country we plan to visit, its current situashun, economical and environmental, its inhabitants—tribes and stuff; even shtisticks, ferchristsake, if I wish him to take me abroad during my vacations. And last, with a leash, I must accompany him to museeeums, until I begin to swoon, just before I get Stendhal sin drome, you know when you see too many paintings and statues, you become kinda crazy and start confusing Peak Asshole with Mowgli Hyena, Van Heck and Matrix, Robin Hood with Save Me Your Dollars—yeah that's Salvador Dali, who was called Avida Dollar by the French, he accumulated so much money during his life, not like poor Van Hop, who sold only one portrait, before he conked out, with a severed ear washmore, and that was thanks to his brother Theo.

Unlike what you are insinuating, Adam—who gave you that name? Do you think you're the father of humanity? In that case, I'm the mother, but we won't get married, coz I'm an independent felinist. Careful about what you say, or I'll spank you real hard in the butt. I don't mind most of my classmates, even if they're no Einsteins or Marie Curie—no the ladder didn't invent curry rice, go to Wikipipi and see who she was and why she earned the Nobel Prize; as long as they behave, but I can't stand those the petty and arrogant bozos, who laugh at others or are plain jealous, like Charlotte de Jerq, who, if you remember, tells everybody she's my friend. Not even in another life!

Albert: I like genuine folk, whether they are workers, farmers and—more rarely—intellectuals. I admire intelligence, but only accompanied with altruism and consideration. I despise journalists, reporters, historians, TV moderators who believe they are superior to others, think only of climbing the steps to fame, and who are politically or ideologically motivated, while they spread lies and poisonous opinions around them. I've had my share of these obnoxious people, especially in France.

Adam: Albert, you are quite open about sexuality in the Zapinette series. Is it your opinion that most young people are mature enough to find your books informative and thought-provoking in constructive ways? And have you or Zapinette ever received comments that these books perhaps deserve an R-rating due to sexual content and Zapinette's occasional "swear word" vernacular?

Zapinette: Looka here Adamo! I dunno how much you knew when you stopped peeing in your pants, but today, thanks to Internet, the movies—where you see men and women with no fig leaf you know where; but also because we get courses on sexual education, very early. Yeah, my teacher doesn't only talk to

168

us about bees in a bonnet. Nobody has complained about my knowledge, and don't confuse me with a setchual pervert, orrr else I'll smack you. I know how babies come about, but I ain't interested at all in them adulterated shenanigans; and growl-ups seem to be obsessed with sex. I saw snippets of their games, by mistake, when Unky Berky switched on the TV, not knowing that the film was X-rated, and frankly, it looks boring like hell. I have much more interesting things to do. Tell me Adamino, what's more vulgar: to say fookin' this or bloomin' that, or to show us how people die in Syria, with their bodies torn to pieces and covered with blood?

Albert: Zapinette has answered in my behalf.

Adam: Zapinette, you seem to have the best of "all worlds": the fun of being able to be childish and playful when you want, and the maturity to understand "adult stuff" (sometimes perhaps even to the point of "knowing too much"). Do you ever feel—like Peter Pan—that you never want to grow up? And will Albert ever allow you to really grow up in your future books?

Zapinette: Peter Pan yourself, and don't mock my lil brother Peter either, he's so adorabbable. Can you imagine me floating in the stratosphere like a damn human butterfly? Well I never! so sayeth Shake'n Pears. My uncle claims that we never know enough. But sometimes I can't stop telling him "enough already", coz I get headaches when he gives me too much information, some of which is bunk, like how much ozone destruction we've had in the last five years, percentage wise. Are we the wiser for it???

Albert: That is up to Zapinette. She may want to stay an eternal know-all chil' baby, which doesn't prevent her from falling in love, like with … Charlie-Kea when she was kidnapped in New York. But I have an inkling that it will remain platonic. If she does want to grow up, she is welcome; but then how will I deal with that situation? Too early to say.

Adam: If Zapinette ever were to become a "First Lady", what country would she most like to be "First Lady" of? Which countries would a "felinist" like Zapinette not like to be a leader of? And why?

Zapinette: A First Lady, me? A lady president maybe, but I don't think I'd like that either, on account of that all presidents lie and have to footsie foot even with allies who stink, in order to avoid additional wars. No, I'd rather study to be a real actress like Meryl Streep, my mentoress, or even become a film director.

Albert: Her response is mine too.

Adam: Today women in the "free world" can live openly as lesbians or bisexuals. Zapinette is appealing to both male and female readers, and has many fans of all genders, races, creeds and sexual expressions. Is it foreseeable that Zapinette will experiment with bisexuality or lesbianism? Does she desire to have children? And will she inherit her mother's hair salon and become a businesswoman-hairdresser, or will she most likely choose another profession? Perhaps as a film actress, or a star in a Broadway play?

Zapinette: Now Adamaccio—yeah that sounds a bit crude, but you have to watch what you're saying. I ain't thinking of becoming any of the things you are suggesting, at least not now, even if I respect everyone, as long as they don't hurt or molest children. I have more important subjects to tackle, and as the French say, 'qui vivra verra'. So what if I get married later on with a Missus! I will let no one interfere with my life, capito! Now, it's kind, intelligent boys, I'm interested in, and they must also be feminists, not necessarily felinists. Do you understand the difference, or must I waste my time explaining it to you? Ok, for $50 I can do it. Is that kosher enough for you?

Albert: Of course, I'm an adult, with sexual needs, while Zapinette has other priorities. Oh, like me, she also dreams of becoming an aviatrix. She has all the time in the world to learn the profession. As for me, it is much too late.

Adam: Thank you very much Zapinette and Albert. We all hope to read many more of your fascinating stories in the near future—and I know that many of us are waiting for some feature films, or a TV-series based on your books.

Zapinette (with Albert nodding his head in agreement): We both say to you, dear Adamino (an endearing name this time): Thanks a ton, mercy beaucoup, mille grazie, and ten forks and ding dong.

PART FOUR

WHEN WORDS ARE INADEQUATE: ALBERT RUSSO AS PHOTOGRAPHER OF THE WORLD

"Art is but a moment of bliss, a lightning cleaving the somber,

never-ending horrors of our world."

— *Albert Russo*

POET AS PHOTOGRAPHER / PHOTOGRAPHER AS POET

ALBERT RUSSO—NOVELIST, ESSAYIST, SHORT STORY WRITER, POET ..... PHOTOGRAPHER.

Of some fifty-five book publications to-date, eighteen of Russo's books are photographic essays. These titles include impressions from travels around the world, quirkiness and humour in human experience, studies of sculptures, autobiographical essays with photography as the medium, and more. Had Russo not had such a passion for art and literature, he would surely have had a fine career as a photojournalist for commercial publishers of travel books, travel guides and travel magazines. However, Russo's inclination towards the artistic and social elements of human predicament and expression, coupled with his love of poetry, has resulted in a myriad of publications which effectively express poetic and literary curiosity through poetry's modern-day "first cousin": photography. I use the word "curiosity" intentionally as Russo never forces his impressions upon us as an expression of "truth", but rather guides us through his own personal experiences and thoughts through visual exposés. Sometimes the progressive order of photographs in some of his books can seem somewhat illogical as Russo presents us with his own "connections" between impressions as he sees them as an artist—rather than grouping photographs in an order that an advertising executive or commercial travel book might choose. This is Russo's prerogative, his perspective ... and an important aspect of his own unique poetic expression.

Some of his photography books are combinations of texts and pictures, and others are without texts. The absence of titles is a bold artistic statement in itself, relying upon the strength and the progression of the photographs themselves to tell the author's/photographer's personal story. Personally, I prefer the books that consist of photographs alone as I do not always relate to the accompanying texts and find them sometimes to be as annoying as I find signatures on the front side of paintings (when the signatures not only do not add to the overall work of art, but actually detract from the viewing experience). But this is a question of personal taste. Having a background both within visual art and poetry, I—like Albert Russo—am capable of understanding the "poetry" in the photographic presentations without explanation or added literary decoration. I think this is true for many (if not most) persons who enjoy photography books as works of art. Russo's photographic essays include, among others: "A poetic biography", "Brussels ride", "Chinese puzzle", "City of lovers", "Granada", "En / in France", "Israel at heart", "Italia nostra", "Mexicana", "New York at heart", "Pasión de España", "Quirk", "Rainbow nature", "Saint-Malo", "Sardinia", "Sri Lanka", and his "Body glorious" and "Norway to Spitzberg". These are almost exclusively full-colour photos ... a medium which Russo plays with combining childlike naiveté and curiosity for the unusual aspects of the "banal", and exciting excursions into nature and the planet's overall cultural diversity, with a broad palette of professional techniques. Russo goes to great pains to mix traditional images with their contemporary partners and counterparts, and to play with exposure, light, filters and clarity/non-clarity in order to exaggerate aspects of the culture and to communicate his own personal experiences and sensations. I would like to see a photographic essay by Albert Russo, in which he translates his interactive communication between photographer/poet and subject to the medium of black and white photography. I am certain that Russo would find even more exciting nuances and enigmatic photographic puzzles through the usage of light, shadows, layers of greyness etc., which would even further enhance his natural highly-effective ability to penetrate beyond picture-taking ... and far, far into the inner energy forms and thoughts of his photographic subjects/objects and their surrounding environment/conditions.

Perhaps the most unusual photographic essay is his "A Poetic Biography", published in 2006. The book is exactly what the title suggests: a collection of photographs of Russo, his family members and friends in various situations and environments, and over a period of several decades. Here Russo includes both photographs of people (colour and some black and white), photographs of letters and telefaxes, telegrams, articles on Russo as an author etc.—all without explanation or commentary. In this way, Russo uses the classic "first person" style of prose-writing to create an almost surrealistic glimpse into the inner reaches of Russo's personality, history, personal life, ambitions and self-identity. The book leaves us with a yearning to discover that personal aspect which Russo has not commented on, but which most other artists and authors usually make no bones about proclaiming ad nauseam: namely, his dreams ... and what his life might have been like otherwise.

Another fun and beautiful photographic exposé is Russo's "Norway to Spitzberg". I have previously reviewed this book and commented: "Albert Russo's photographic essay illustrating a cruise ship voyage with the Costa Atlantica («La città ideale») along the coast of Norway, from the city of Bergen (birthplace of composer Edvard Grieg) to the top of the globe (Spitzberg) is fascinating not only because of his realizing the full circle of «post-post-realism» in modern photography, but also because Mr. Russo transforms the tourist «photo-stalker» experience into the creation of a professional visual compendium—combining dramatic and magnificent seascapes, fjordscapes and landscapes with the intimacy of still lifes, the humanity of people at work and play, and in their quiet, alone moments, as well as the extremities of fauna, and indigenous peoples (and their cultural expressions and living environments). It is not difficult to understand that Mr. Russo is also an accomplished poet and a master of prose-writing. The stories he tells in this photographic essay are not a mere show of proficiency as regards each individual work of art, but rather a dance of images as vivid as an operatic performance—full of passion, drama, silences, humour and music. Mr. Russo has employed a Canon digital Ixus 55—5.0 megapixels camera, with 3x optical zoom. His «eye» for discerning, and his talent for capturing the «photographic moment», the mastery of light and clarity vs. slight distortion etc. is a testament to his delicious sense of artistry, as well as his empathy for the experience of being human."

Out of curiosity, I took contact with Albert Russo to ask him to comment on his love for photography. Here are his comments:

"In response to your question: I've always liked photography, from my adolescent years in Africa; actually I loved filming too and my 8mm or super 8mm films looked more like stills than films. People would complain telling me:

'Oh God, five minutes on the same object, flower, trees, landscape, whatever, enough already!' Ever since my African days I've been taking photos with all kinds of cameras: from the standard Kodak box, to the famous German Minox, to the Fujica ST-605 (a wonderful camera that accompanied me everywhere)—often using the Rexastar lens for close-ups (1:3.5—f-135mm), alternately with the smaller but very friendly Minolta 70W Riva zoom, and now with the Canon digital Ixus 55. I have probably forgotten a few other cameras I have had. Oh, I used to take many colour slides in Africa (which I still have tucked away somewhere, and should one day soon think of printing the best of them). Poetry and photography? They are always closely related. A good picture tells a thousand things to the beholder if he/she pays attention to it, and the 'right' word suggests a thousand other things. That is why I never like to simply write captions under my photos. Actually, now I do not wish to write anything at all. The photo must speak to you on its own."

In conclusion, I would recommend that art photography and poetry enthusiasts take note of this talented artist. As one who has reviewed his collected poetry and read many of his novels, short stories and essays, I can attest that his literary talent complements his photographic expression. Albert Russo is artistically self-integrated in all of his creative disciplines.

EPILOGUE

.

PRISONERS OF OUR TONGUE

a haiku sequence by Albert Russo

don't generalize

you oversimplify things

so I'm often told

then I get mad

and hit people where it hurts

hurling words at them

you exaggerate

you're too unconventional

for your own good

all of a sudden

I realize that we are all

in the same boat

I'm fighting in vain

the moment we open our mouths

we are trapped

no way of getting out

unless, unless we keep quiet

the solution? SILENCE!

AWARDS & BIBLIOGRAPHY

LIST OF ALBERT RUSSO'S MAJOR AWARDS IN ENGLISH AND IN FRENCH

Médaille de bronze for French poetry written in 1971, Prix Colette and Prix de la Liberté for 'La Pointe du Diable' (later renamed 'Le Cap des Illusions'), Cannes, 1972. The American Society of Writers Fiction Award, The British Diversity Short Story Award, the Azsacra Poetry award ($500, Taj Mahal Review), best UNICEF 2013 Award for poetry, plus dozens of awards from around the world for essays, short stories and poetry. Albert Russo was awarded the 'Diplôme de la Francophonie', along with a number of his African peers, by Europoésie, Paris, in May 2017, AFRICA being the theme of that particular year.

BIBLIOGRAPHY OF ALBERT RUSSO'S PUBLISHED NOVELS

La Pointe du diable, novel, Pierre Deméyère éditions, Brussels, 1972

Mosaïque Newyorkaise, novella, Editions de l'Athanor, Paris, France, 1975

Sang Mêlé ou ton fils Léopold, novel, Editions du Griot, Paris, France, 1990

- France Loisirs, Paris, France, 1991

- Ginkgo éditeur, Paris, France, 2007

Le Cap des illusions, novel, Editions du Griot, Paris, France, 1991

Eclipse sur le lac Tanganyica, novel, Le Nouvel Athanor, Paris, 1994

- Element Uitgevers, Dutch edition, 1996

Zapinette Vidéo, novel, Éditions Hors Commerce, Paris, France, 1996

L'amant de mon père 1, (journal parisien) novel, Nouvel Athanor, Paris, 2000

Zapinette chez les Belges, novel, Editions Hors Commerce, Paris, France, 2001

Zapinette à New York, novel, Éditions Hors Commerce, Paris, 2001

L'amante di mio padre Edizioni Libreria Croce, Rome, 2002

L'ancêtre noire, novel, Éditions Hors Commerce, Paris, 2003

L'amant de mon père II:Journal romain, novel, Éditions Hors Commerce, Paris, 2003

L'amant de mon père II:Journal romain, novel, édition de poche, Paris, 2003

The Benevolent American in the Heart of Darkness , 3 novels set in the former Belgian Congo and Ruanda-Urundi: Mixed Blood, The Black Ancestor, Eclipse over Lake Tanganyika, Xlibris, USA, 2004

Oh Zaperetta, 3 novels, Xlibris, USA, 2005

La Tour Shalom, Editions Hors Commerce, Paris, France, 2005

Sangue Misto, Coniglio editore, Italian edition, 2008

Sangue Misto, Elliot editore, Italian edition, 2016

Shalom Tower Syndrome, novel, Libreria Croce Editore, 2008

Exils Africains, novel, Ginkgo Editeur, Paris, France, 2010

Zulu Zapy wins the Rainbow Nation, novel co-published by Cyberwit.net (India) and Poetry Printery (South Africa), 2010

Léodine l'Africaine, novel, Ginkgo Editeur, Paris, France, 2011

Gosh Zapinette (Series of 7 novels), Imago Press, USA 2012

Io, Hans, figlio di nazisti, novel, Edizioni Libreria Croce, Rome, 2013

Zapinette la Parigina, novel, Edizioni Libreria Croce, Rome, 2013

Zapinette la Spaghettona nel paese di Mandela, 2 novels, Edizioni Libreria Croce, Rome, 2013

Dopo il gay Parigi, Zapinette viene rapita a New York, 2 novels, Edizioni Libreria Croce, Roma, 2014

The African Quatuor, four novels, e-book, l'Aleph, Sweden, 2014

Zapinette Baguette e Tagliatelle, 3 novels, l'Aleph, Sweden, 2014

Des Princes et des Dieux (formerly Eclipse sur le lac Tanganyika), Ginkgo éditeur, Paris, 2015, print and e-book

i-Sraeli Syndrome, novel, l'Aleph, Sweden, 2014

Zapinette Burqa Burquette in Terra Santa, 2 novels, Edizioni Libreria Croce, Roma, 2015

The African Quatuor, 4 African novels, l'Aleph, Sweden, 2015, e-book, including Princes and Gods, Eur-African Exiles, Adopted by an American Homosexual in the Belgian Congo and Léodine of the Belgian Congo: all four are available individually in both print and e-books

L'amant de mon père, journal parisien et journal romain, Editions Textes Gais (TG), Paris, print and e-books, 2015

Zapinette—6 volumes, Editions Textes Gais (TG), Paris, e-books, 2016:

Zapinette et son tonton aux Champs Elysées

Zapinette et son tonton chez les Belges

Zapinette et son tonton à la Gay Pride

Zapinette et son tonton découvrent l'Italie

Zapinette et son tonton découvrent New York

Zapinette et son tonton au pays des Zoulous

Gosh Zapinette! series of 9 novels, cyberwit.net, India, 2016

Mémoires d'un fils de nazis, Culture Commune, TG, Paris, e-book, 2017

His stories, essays and poetry have appeared in hundreds of magazines on the five continents, the major ones being: Playboy, Cosmopolitan, the International Herald Tribune (NYT & Washington Post), The Literary Review, World Literature Today, Archeology Impulse (Canada) Libération, The Times of Israel, Ambit, New Hope International, the Taj Mahal Review, Poets of the World / Poetas del mundo (Chile), Poet Printery (South Africa) …

Some of his works have been translated into more than 15 languages around the world.

BIBLIOGRAPHY OF ALBERT RUSSO'S POETRY, SHORT STORY AND ESSAY COLLECTIONS

POETRY, SOME WITH PHOTOS BY THE AUTHOR

Dans la nuit bleu-fauve / Futureyes, poetry, bilingual (English and French), with ink drawings, Le Nouvel Athanor, Paris, 1992

Kaleidoscope, The Plowman, Canada, 1993

Painting the Tower of Babel, poetry, New Hope International, GB, 1996.

Poetry and Peanuts, poetry, Cherrybite Publications, GB, 1997

The Crowded World of Solitude, Volume 2, the collected poems, some of it bilingual (English and French), Xlibris, USA, 2005.

Tour du monde de la poésie gay : Voyage(s) facétieux d'Albert Russo, Editions Hors Commerce, Paris, 2005

Gaytude, poetic journey around the world, bilingual (English / French), Albert Russo and Adam Donaldson Powell, Xlibris, USA, 2009.

Embers under my skin, poetry, Imago Press (USA), 2012: two editions: CreateSpace / Amazon and Blurb Inc., USA

SHORT STORY AND ESSAY COLLECTIONS

The Crowded World of Solitude,Volume 1, the collected stories and essays, Xlibris, USA, 2005.

Beyond the Great Water, Vol.1, Collected stories, Domhan Books, USA/GB, 2001.

Unmasking Hearts, Vol.2, Collected stories, Domhan Books, USA/GB, 2001.

The Age of the Pearl, Vol.3, Collected stories, Domhan Books, USA/GB, 2001.

Le Règne du Caméléon, long story and photos, Imago Press (USA), 2012

MEMOIRS AND BIOGRAPHIES,
SOME WITH PHOTOS BY THE AUTHOR

A poetic biography / Biographie poétique in 2 volumes, Xlibris, USA, 2005

Crystals in a shock wave, nonfiction, Blurb Inc. & Createspace/Amazon, 2012

Mother beloved, Mamica mia, nonfiction, Create space/Amazon, USA, 2013

Ode to Mamica mia, Mother beloved, nonfiction, Createspace/Amazon, 2013

Au naturel / born naked, Createspace/Amazon, 2013

Call me Chameleon, 1000-page memoir, with photos, l'Aleph, Sweden, 2015

MISC. / MÉLANGES

Incandescences, mélange of novellas, stories and poems, Promotion & Edition, Paris, 1970

Eclats de malachite, novel, Editions Pierre Deméyère, Brussels, Belgium, 1971

Venitian Thresholds, Bone & Flesh Publications, USA, 1995

Boundaries of Exile / Conditions of Hope, bilingual (English and French) by Albert Russo and Martin Tucker, Confrontation Press (Long Island University, NY), 2009

BIBLIOGRAPHY OF ALBERT RUSSO'S ZAPINETTE SERIES

Zapinette Vidéo, novel, Éditions Hors Commerce, Paris, France, 1996

Zapinette chez les Belges, novel, Editions Hors Commerce, Paris, France, 2001

Zapinette à New York, novel, Éditions Hors Commerce, Paris, 2001

Oh Zaperetta, 3 novels, Xlibris, USA, 2005

Zulu Zapy wins the Rainbow Nation, novel co-published by Cyberwit.net (India) and Poetry Printery (South Africa), 2010

Gosh Zapinette (Series of 7 novels), Imago Press, USA 2012

Zapinette la Parigina, novel, Edizioni Libreria Croce, Rome, 2013

Zapinette la Spaghettona nel paese di Mandela, 2 novels, Edizioni Libreria Croce, Rome, 2013

Dopo il gay Parigi, Zapinette viene rapita a New York, 2 novels, Edizioni Libreria Croce, Roma, 2014

Zapinette Baguette e Tagliatelle, 3 novels, l'Aleph, Sweden, 2014

Zapinette Burqa Burquette in Terra Santa, 2 novels, Edizioni Libreria Croce, Roma, 2015

Zapinette—6 volumes, Editions Textes Gais (TG), Paris, e-books, 2016:

    Zapinette et son tonton aux Champs Elysées

    Zapinette et son tonton chez les Belges

    Zapinette et son tonton à la Gay Pride

    Zapinette et son tonton découvrent l'Italie

    Zapinette et son tonton découvrent New York

    Zapinette et son tonton au pays des Zoulous

https://goo.gl/QMucWL

Gosh Zapinette! series of 9 novels, cyberwit.net, India, 2016

—୦ஒ—

ALBERT RUSSO'S PHOTOBOOKS AND VIDEO MOVIES

ROMAdiva, Xlibris, USA, 2004

Mexicana, Xlibris, USA, 2005

Sri Lanka / Serendib, Xlibris, USA, 2005

A poetic biography / Biographie poétique, 2 volumes, Xlibris, USA, 2005

AfricaSoul, Xlibris, USA, 2006

En/In France, Xlibris, USA, 2006

Saint Malo, with love, Xlibris, USA, 2006

Body glorious, Xlibris, USA, 2006

Sardinia, Xlibris, USA, 2006

Bruxelles au galop / Brussels ride, Xlibris, USA, 2006

Granada, Costa del Sol & Ronda, Xlibris, USA, 2007

City of Lovers—City of Wonder, Paris—New York, Xlibris, USA, 2007

Italia Nostra, Xlibris, USA, 2007

Israel at heart, Xlibris, USA, 2007

Italia Nostra, Xlibris, USA, 2007

Pasión de España, Xlibris, USA, 2007

RainbowNature, Xlibris, USA, 2007

Viennese kaleidoscope, Blurb Inc., USA, 2007

Quirks / Éclats, Xlibris, USA, 2008

Norway to Spitzberg, Blurb Inc., USA, 2008

Noël à / in Paris, Blurb Inc., USA, 2008

Eilat, Petra & Tel Aviv, Blurb Inc., USA, 2008

Celestial blues, Blurb Inc., USA, 2010

Visions of Venice, Blurb Inc., USA, 2010

Senegal Live, Blurb Inc., USA, 2010

Animal Kinship, Blurb Inc., USA, 2010

Mermaids of the Baltic Sea, Blurb Inc., USA, 2010

China Forever, Blurb Inc., USA, 2010

Expressive Romans, Blurb Inc., USA, 2010

France: Art, Humour & Nature, Blurb Inc., USA, 2010

Garden Delights, Blurb Inc., USA, 2010

In the air, on the ground & on the water, Blurb Inc., USA, 2010

Symphony in Hands major, Blurb Inc., USA, 2010

Living Objects / Objets-Miroir, Blurb Inc., USA, 2011

Israel / Jordan / Palestine, Blurb Inc., USA, 2012

Venice, Empress of the Seas, Blurb Inc., USA, 2012

Oriental gems, Blurb Inc., USA, 2012

A myriad tales, vol.1, Createspace/Amazon, USA, 2012

A myriad tales, vol.2, Createspace/Amazon, USA, 2012

Fotoripples, vol.1,2 & 3, Createspace/Amazon, USA, 2012

Rome, my sibling, my empress, Createspace/Amazon, 2013

Seven living Splendors, B&W photos, Createspace/Amazon, 2013

Tel Aviv, the rainbow city, Createspace/Amazon, 2015

LITERARY WORKS MADE INTO VIDEO MOVIES

1. Watch Novel EUR-AFRICAN EXILES / EXILS AFRICAINS both written originally by Albert Russo turned into movie by Wildsound feature film— producer Matthew Toffolo: SANDRO'S NOTEBOOK—EUR-AFRICAN EXILES. See: https://goo.gl/L0ZNMT

2. ADOPTED BY AN AMERICAN HOMOSEXUAL IN THE BELGIAN CONGO by Albert Russo, a Wildsound feature film, English book by l'Aleph—Wisehouse Publishing, French book: SANG MÊLÉ by Ginkgo Éditeur, both originally written by Russo, SANGUE MISTO, by Elliot, Rome, (Italian translation). See the whole video: https://goo.gl/Bufxjm

ADAM DONALDSON POWELL (Norway) is a multilingual author, literary critic, art photography critic; and a professional visual artist. He has published several literary books (including collections of poetry, short stories, and novellas, two science fiction novels, and essays); as well as numerous works in international literary publications—on several continents. He writes in English, Spanish, French and Norwegian. He has previously authored theatrical works performed onstage, and he has read his poetry at venues in New York City (USA), Oslo (Norway), Buenos Aires (Argentina), and Kathmandu (Nepal). His book "Gaytude" (co-authored with Albert Russo) won the 2009 National Indie Excellence Award in the category gay/lesbian non-fiction. Powell was also the winner of the Azsacra International Poetry Award in 2008, and the recipient of a Norwegian Foreign Ministry travel stipend for authors in 2005.

Other works by Adam Donaldson Powell:

Entre Nous et Eux: contes de fées pour adultes

Jisei: death poems and daily reflections of a person with AIDS

The tunnel at the end of time

Gaytude: a poetic journey around the world

2014: the life and adventures of an incarnated angel

Critical Essays

Le Paradis (Paradise)

Rapture: endings of space and time

Three-legged Waltz

Collected poems and stories

Arcana and other archetypes

Notes of a Madman

Lightning Source UK Ltd.
Milton Keynes UK
UKOW04f1914231017
311527UK00001B/29/P